Unlocking the Power of Language

Research-Based Strategies for Language Development

Debra J. Coffey
Alice F. Snyder

Kendall Hunt
publishing company
4050 Westmark Drive • P O Box 1840 • Dubuque IA 52004-1840

This book is dedicated to the creative and innovative students of
Kennesaw State University.

Cover credits:
gold letters:
Image © ivn3da 2009, under license from Shutterstock, Inc.

keyhole:
Image © Nikolay Okhitin 2009, under license from Shutterstock, Inc.

alphabet letters (back cover):
Image © digitalife 2009, under license from Shutterstock, Inc.

Printed in the United States of America
10 9 8 7 6 5 4 3 2 1

Contents

ABCs of Literacy

The Author's Chair

The strategies in this book are designed to unlock the power of language. Our goal is to present research-based strategies that amplify literacy instruction. These strategies provide educators with tools that empower children to explore the **alphabetic principle**, delve into quality literature by focusing on the **author's message,** and share their own writing from the **author's chair**. When students sit in the author's chair to share their writing, they experience the final stage of the writing process. Through this experience they synthesize their knowledge of alphabetic concepts and literature to share their own creative messages.

English is an alphabetic language with 26 letters, 44 phonemes, and over 500 different spellings that represent those phonemes. Children initially develop **phonemic awareness** as they become familiar with the smallest units of sound. Phonemic awareness is enhanced as they listen to stories. As children develop phonemic awareness, they should be able to blend and segment phonemes. The **alphabetic principle** focuses on the ability to associate these sounds with letters. As students learn to associate these sounds with letters, they begin to use these letters to form words. During this process, research-based strategies for **phonics** help children to see the connections between sounds and letters as they learn about words in the context of enjoyable literature. The strategies in this book highlight ways to guide children as they explore the **author's message** and build enthusiasm for literature.

Exploring the Author's Message with the Author's Chair Strategy

- A student author reads a personal draft or edited composition in a special chair.

- The author may also share illustrations of the composition with the audience.

- Then the author requests comments from the audience.

- The teacher may model and guide responses while seeking to encourage the author.

- Comments focus upon favorite events, characters, or particularly interesting and notable uses of language.

- The author or members of the audience may seek clarification and suggestions.

- Then audience offers suggestions and discusses the author's message.

This is one example of the research-based strategies featured throughout this text. We seek to unlock the power of language by using a balanced approach to highlight strategies for developing word knowledge, exploring literature, and guiding tutorial instruction. The text is organized by the letters of the **alphabet** for easy access to literacy resources.

Author Studies

Notable Picture Book Authors and Illustrators

As children master the alphabetic principle and experience the power of language, author studies bring favorite authors into the classroom. Children are curious about the authors who create their beloved books, and author displays promote the magic of reading. Pictures of authors on tri-fold displays, examples of items from books, and exploration of authors' websites bring books to life in dynamic ways.

Janet and Alan Ahlberg	Mary Hoffman
Jim Aylesworth	Pat Hutchins
Molly Bang	Susan Jeffers
Jan Brett	William Joyce
Marc Brown	Ezra Jack Keats
Debbi Chocolate	Leo Lionni
Eric Carle	Anita Lobel
Donald Crews	Arnold Lobel
Nina Crews	Bill Martin, Jr.
Pat Cummings	Pat Mora
Jamie Lee Curtis	Laura Numeroff
Tomie dePaola	Anne Rockwell
Lois Ehlert	Marisabino Russo
Ian Falconer	Cynthia Rylant
Denise Fleming	Eileen Spinelli
Mem Fox	Janet Stevens
Stephen Gammell	"Dr. Seuss"
Gail Gibbons	Rosemary Wells
Kevin Henkes	Vera B. Williams
Tana Hoban	Audrey & Don Wood
Yumi Heo	Paul O. Zelinsky

Author Biography
Planning Sheet

About the Author

Childhood

Background

Favorites

Books and Media for Illustrations

Alphabet Song
and Alphabet Scrapbooks

Identifying Letters

Children need to learn the letters of the alphabet in proper order, and they also need to learn how to identify letters in the context of words. Some children will have difficulty making the link from saying the letters of the alphabet to identifying letters in combination with other letters to form words. To help them learn letters in the context of words, point out letters in Big Books, the Morning Message, or their names. Guiding children to identify letters in print will help them learn how to read.

DIRECTIONS

1. Choose a story, Morning Message, or one of the children's names to teach children how to identify letters. The story can be one that you read to the children, a dictated story, or a Big Book with which the children are familiar. Be sure the material is large enough for all children to see.

2. Read the story, message, or name aloud to the children. Then have the children read it with you.

3. Place several letter cards on the table in front of you. Have a child choose a letter from the stack.

4. Have the child identify the letter. If the letter is a *d,* for example, the child should say *d.*

5. Ask the children to locate any letter in the story that matches the letter chosen by the child. In this case, children should look for the letter *d.* Have one child at a time come up to point out examples of the letter in the story. If the story does not have that particular letter, the child should replace the letter in the stack and choose another letter.

6. Repeat until all of the letters in the stack have been chosen.

7. Do this activity regularly so children are able to identify the letters easily.

Alphabet Scrapbooks

Children learn about letters as they have repeated opportunities to identify, discuss, read, and write them (Bear, Invernizzi, Templeton, & Johnston, 2004). An ongoing activity that helps children learn letters and connect them to words is making alphabet scrapbooks. In this activity, children create a page for each letter of the alphabet by writing the letter, drawing pictures, and cutting and pasting photos of things that begin with the letter. For children who are more advanced in letter knowledge (or as the school year progresses), they can also write high-frequency words that begin with the target letter. The alphabet scrapbook can also be used as a resource—a type of picture dictionary—as children read and write.

DIRECTIONS

1. Prepare a blank scrapbook for each child by stapling or comb-binding together 14 sheets of heavy construction paper or card stock. This scrapbook will allow one page for each letter as well as a front and back cover.

2. As you teach and review specific letters, have children complete the corresponding page in their alphabet scrapbook.

3. For the first alphabet scrapbook page, model the process for children. For example, for the letter *m* you might say the following.

   I am going to make the *m* page for my alphabet scrapbook. First, I'm going to write a capital *M* and a lower case *m* at the top of the page. Next, I'm going to think of things I can draw that start with the letter *m*. Let's see, I can draw a monkey and a man. In this magazine, I see a picture of a muffin so I'll cut that out and use my glue stick to add it to the page. I wonder if I know any words that I can write that begin with the letter *m*. Oh yes, I know how to write *my* and *mom*. I'll add those to my alphabet scrapbook page.

4. Provide children with markers, magazines, scissors, and glue sticks to complete their scrapbook page.

5. As children complete a page in their alphabet scrapbook, provide time for them to share and discuss the letter and the pictures and words they included on their page.

6. Provide time for children to review pages they previously completed in their alphabet scrapbooks as a way of reinforcing their alphabet knowledge.

Alphabet Knowledge

OVERVIEW	This assessment contains uppercase and lowercase letters of the alphabet in nonsequential order to help assess letter-naming ability. Lowercase *a* and *g* appear in both manuscript and print forms. There are two forms of the test. You may want to use Form 1 at the beginning of the year and Form 2 later in the year.
MATERIALS NEEDED	1. Child's copy, either Form 1 (page 7) or Form 2 (page 9): two 5″ × 8″ cards 2. A copy of the Record Sheet (page 8 or page 10) that corresponds to the form selected for use
PROCEDURES	1. Duplicate the appropriate Record Sheet. 2. Place the alphabet page before the child. Use the 5″ × 8″ cards to block off everything but the line being read. If necessary, point to each letter. Say, "Here are some letters. I want to see how many you know." Encourage the child to say "pass" or "skip it" if a particular letter is not known. Stop if the child becomes frustrated or has little or no knowledge of the letters. 3. As the child responds, use the Record Sheet to note correct (+) responses. When responses are incorrect, record the actual response or *DK* (child doesn't know) above the stimulus letter. If the child self-corrects, write *s/c*; self-corrections can be made at any time. Some sample markings for the letter o are given below.

Marking	Meaning of Marking	Marking	Meaning of Marking
+ O	Identified correct	C O	Said C for O
DK O	Don't know	C s/c O	Said C for O but self-corrected

SCORING AND INTERPRETATION	Count the correct number of responses for the uppercase letters and the lowercase letters. Self-corrections are counted as correct. Note the scores in the boxes on the Record Sheet on page 8 or 10. Based on the number of correct responses and your observations, make a judgment about the child's alphabet knowledge. Unknown letters or incorrect responses may help form the basis for instruction. Refer to Section 3.1.

B   T   R   Z   F   N   K

X   V   I   M   J   D   L

Y   Q   W   C   U   A

O   H   S   E   G   P

s   d   o   a   k   w   g

l   u   r   t   q   h   y

i   p   v   f   n   z   g

b   x   e   c   j   m   a

Form 1—Alphabet Knowledge—Child's Copy

7

RECORD SHEET

Form 1

Alphabet Knowledge

Name _____ Date _____

Teacher's Directions   6
Child's Copy   7

BRIEF DIRECTIONS

Present the alphabet sheet to the child. Use 5″ × 8″ cards to block off everything but the line being read. If necessary, point to each letter with a finger. Then say, "Here are some letters. I want to see how many you know." Place a plus (+) above correctly identified letters. Record the child's responses for incorrect letters. Total correct responses and record the score in the boxes. Note that lowercase *a* and *g* appear in both manuscript and print forms.

B	T	R	Z	F	N	K
X	V	I	M	J	D	L
Y	Q	W	C	U	A	
O	H	S	E	G	P	

☐ **Total Correct**

s	d	o	a	k	w	g
l	u	r	t	q	h	y
i	p	v	f	n	z	g
b	x	e	c	j	m	a

☐ **Total Correct**

I   S   K   H   Q   V   L

A   G   P   J   N   D   M

T   C   Z   E   F   U

B   O   X   Y   R   W

r   x   z   k   t   e   y

w   q   c   g   h   m   a

i   p   s   v   d   l   j

u   o   f   b   a   n   g

Form 2—Alphabet Knowledge—Child's Copy

9

RECORD SHEET

Form 2

Alphabet Knowledge

Name _____ Date _____

| Teacher's Directions | 6 |
| Child's Copy | 9 |

BRIEF DIRECTIONS

Present the alphabet sheet to the child. Use 5″ × 8″ cards to block off everything but the line being read. If necessary, point to each letter with a finger. Then say, "Here are some letters. I want to see how many you know." Place a plus (+) above correctly identified letters. Record the child's responses for incorrect letters. Total correct responses and record the score in the boxes. Note that lowercase *a* and *g* appear in both manuscript and print forms.

I	S	K	H	Q	V	L
A	G	P	J	N	D	M
T	C	Z	E	F	U	
B	O	X	Y	R	W	

☐ **Total Correct**

r	x	z	k	t	e	y
w	q	c	g	h	m	a
i	p	s	v	d	l	j
u	o	f	b	a	n	g

☐ **Total Correct**

Biography of Reading Experiences

Early Reading

Current Reading

Future Goals

Brainstorming

Brainstorming allows children to share what they already know about a topic. This strategy is completed in a group setting; therefore, children who have little or no background knowledge about the topic can benefit from hearing what other children share. During this process, an idea shared by one child will often trigger a related idea for other children. By building and activating their background knowledge, children will be more prepared to understand and remember what they read or what is read to them.

DIRECTIONS

1. Once you have selected a topic for study, present the key word to children by writing it on a piece of chart paper. For example, if you are going to begin a unit on the ocean, write the word *ocean* on chart paper. Draw a circle around the word and be sure to leave space around it to record the children's ideas.

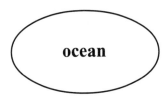

2. Tell children that you want them to share all of the things that come to mind when they hear the word *ocean*. Explain that this process is called brainstorming and that you welcome all responses.

3. Provide time for the children to share their responses as you write them on chart paper.

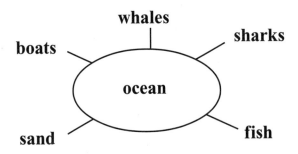

4. After children have had a chance to share their ideas, explain that brainstorming is a great way to prepare for reading.

5. Tell the children that they will be reading books and doing activities related to the ocean. Explain that some of their brainstormed ideas may be covered in the unit and that they will also learn new information on oceans. You may want to revisit the brainstormed ideas during the course of the unit to confirm existing ideas and to add new ideas.

Center Ideas

1. Create an alphabet center in your classroom. Stock the center with plastic letters for word building, letters to trace, alphabet puzzles and games, alphabet books, alphabet stamps, and alphabet flash cards. Allow children time to use the materials in the center on a regular basis.

2. Place a layer of sand or salt in a small container. Have children trace the letters of the alphabet in the sand or salt.

3. Play Letter Bingo. Give each child a card filled with letters of the alphabet and markers to cover the letters. Call a letter and hold up a card with the letter on it. Have children find the letter on their Bingo cards. The first child to cover a row gets Bingo.

4. Create an alphabet path on the floor of your room. Write each letter of the alphabet on a large piece of construction paper. Laminate the pieces of paper, randomly arrange them around your room, and tape them to the floor. Have students walk on the alphabet path saying the letters of the alphabet as they walk.

5. Distribute letter cards to each child. Give each child one card. Call out a letter. Ask the child holding that letter to stand and repeat the name of the letter. Then ask children to say a word that begins with that letter.

6. Provide the children with letter snacks. As you introduce a letter, give children a snack whose name begins with that letter. For example, when you teach the letter *a*, provide each child with a piece of apple.

7. Place a handful of alphabet cereal on a napkin on each child's desk. Have the children sort the cereal letters in alphabetical order. Give children plain round or square cereal to mark the place of letters that are not in the cereal pile. Tell children that if they have more than one of the same letter, they should place the duplicate letters in a row.

8. Write a letter on the chalkboard with a wet sponge or paintbrush. Have children call out the name of the letter before the water evaporates and the letter disappears. Children can also practice writing particular letters with a wet sponge or paintbrush on the chalkboard or on small slates.

9. Distribute copies of newspapers or pages from magazines to each child. Identify a letter and have children circle the letter or use a highlighter marker to show where they find it on a page.

10. Spell out a child's name with letter cards or plastic letters. Use all uppercase letters. Have the child use lowercase letters to match the uppercase letters. Scramble the top row and have the child unscramble the letters to form the correct spelling of the name.

11. Create letter posters by brainstorming words that start with a specific letter. After introducing a letter, have children think of words that start with that letter. If children are unable to correctly identify words beginning with that letter, provide several words for them. Write the words with different color markers or crayons. Display the posters in the classroom or bind them into a class alphabet book.

12. Place a set of five to seven pairs of letter cards face down on a table. You should have two cards for each letter. Have children turn over two cards at a time saying the names of the letters. If the cards match, children keep them. If the cards do not match, have children replace the cards. The object is to match pairs of alphabet cards.

Caption Reading

OVERVIEW	Caption Reading will assess the child's ability to read a brief story with helpful picture clues. This is a helpful assessment to use with children who are just beginning to read.
MATERIALS NEEDED	1. The page in this book containing the caption story, either Form 1 (page 15) or Form 2 (page 18) 2. A copy of the Record Sheet that corresponds to the form selected for use, either Form 1 (pages 16–17) or Form 2 (pages 19–20).
PROCEDURES	1. Show the child the page containing the story. 2. Invite the child to look at frames of the story (pictures and text) in order as numbered. 3. Then ask the child to read the story aloud. Say, "I want you to read the story to me." As the student reads, mentally note any miscues or record them on the appropriate page of the Record Sheet. 4. If the child has difficulty reading the story, have the child listen while you read it aloud. Say, "Listen to me read the story. Then I will want you to read it to me." After your reading, invite the child to read. 5. Encourage the child to talk about the story with you.
SCORING AND INTERPRETATION	Informally note the miscues the child made, the degree of fluency, and other behaviors on the Record Sheet. If the child was able to read the captions, you can informally analyze fluency, miscues, and overall engagement with the task. If you read the story first, evaluate the degree to which the child was able to memorize and repeat the text. Be alert for how the child uses language as you talk about the story.

1

The cat sleeps.

2

The dog sleeps.

3

The bird sleeps.

4

The baby sleeps.

Form 1—Caption Reading—Child's Copy

RECORD SHEET

Form 1

Caption Reading

Name _____ Date _____

The cat sleeps.

The dog sleeps.

The bird sleeps.

The baby sleeps.

QUALITATIVE JUDGMENTS OF READING

If the child read the story, check the statement that best describes the child's reading.

_____ The child's reading is an exact match with the text.

_____ The child's reading closely matches the text.

_____ The child's reading is somewhat related to the text but is based on the illustrations.

_____ The child's reading is related mostly to the illustrations.

If you read the story first, check the statement that best describes the child's reading.

_____ The child used memory to read the text with high accuracy.

_____ The child used memory and illustrations to read the text with fair accuracy.

_____ The child did not seem to remember your reading and relied almost entirely on the illustrations to read the text.

(continues)

RECORD SHEET

Form 1

Caption Reading (continued)

Record your overall qualitative judgment of reading with an X on the continuum located on this record sheet.

	Not Evident Low Seldom Weak Poor		Some		Evident High Always Strong Excellent

Other Reading Behaviors

Retelling

Reads left to right

Reads top to bottom

Demonstrates letter-sound relationships

Uses monitoring (rereads, corrects)

Points to correct words (if requested by you)

Engagement

Confidence as a reader

Observations, Comments, Notes, and Insights

1

The frog sits.

2

The frog eats.

3

The frog jumps.

4

The frog swims.

Form 2—Caption Reading—Child's Copy

18

RECORD SHEET

Form 2

Caption Reading

Name _____ Date _____

The frog sits.

The frog eats.

The frog jumps.

The frog swims.

QUALITATIVE JUDGMENTS OF CAPTION READING

If the child read the story, check the statement that best describes the child's reading.

_____ The child's reading is an exact match with the text.

_____ The child's reading closely matches the text.

_____ The child's reading is somewhat related to the text but is based on the illustrations.

_____ The child's reading is related mostly to the illustrations.

If you read the story first, check the statement that best describes the child's reading.

_____ The child used memory to read the text with high accuracy.

_____ The child used memory and illustrations to read the text with fair accuracy.

_____ The child did not seem to remember your reading and relied almost entirely on the illustrations to read the text.

(continues)

RECORD SHEET

Form 2

Caption Reading (continued)

Record your overall qualitative judgment of reading with an X on the continuum located on this record sheet.

	Not Evident Low Seldom Weak Poor		Some	Evident High Always Strong Excellent

Other Reading Behaviors

Retelling

Reads left to right

Reads top to bottom

Demonstrates letter-sound relationships

Uses monitoring (rereads, corrects)

Points to correct words (if requested by you)

Engagement

Confidence as a reader

Observations, Comments, Notes, and Insights

Concepts of Print Assessment

For this assessment, sit with the student in a quiet place, and use a short picture book from your classroom. The print should be large enough and the words spaced far enough apart that you can easily see where a child is pointing. The book should also have a variety of punctuation marks.

1. **Does the student know the concept of front of the book?**
   Hand book to the student in a vertical position, spine towards child.

   Say, **"Show me the front of this book."**
   Check the box if answer is correct.

2. **Does the student know that the print, not the picture, is the part to be read?**
   Open to the first page of text. There should be a picture on this page.

   Say, **"I will read this book to you. Show me where to read."**
   Check the box if student points to first word on top left of page.

3. **Does the student know which way to read?**
   Turn to the second page of the book.

   Say, **"Point to where I start reading."**
   Check the box if student points to print somewhere on the first page.

4. **Does the student know that print is read from left to right?**
   Say, **"Which way do I go?"**
   Check the box if student moves finger from left to right.

5. **Does the student know at the end of the line to return to the next line?**
   Say, **"Where do I go after that?"**
   Check the box if student "return sweeps" to the left.

Reprinted with permission from *An Observation Survey of Early Literacy* by Marie M. Clay. Copyright © 2003 by Marie M. Clay. Published by Heinemann, Portsmouth, NH. All rights reserved.

6. **Does the student have one-to-one match with voice to print?**

☐ Say, **"Point to the words as I read."**

Check the box if student matches your voice to the print as you read.

7. **Does the student understand the concept of first and last?**

Turn to a new page.

Say, **"Show me the first part of this story."**

☐ Say, **"Show me the last part of this story."**

Check the box if student points to any of the following combinations:

the first and last words on a line

the first and last words in a sentence

the first and last words on a page

the first and last words in the book

8. **Does the student know that the left page is read before the right page?**

Turn the page so that there is a left and right page to read.

☐ Say, **"Where do I start reading?"**

Check the box if student points to the left page.

9. **Does the student know the meaning of a question mark?**

Point to a question mark in the text.

☐ Say, **"What is this for?"**

Check the box if student says, "question mark" or "when you ask something."

10. **Does the student know the meaning of a period?**

Point to a period in the text.

☐ Say, **"What is this for?"**

Check the box if student says "period" or at the end of the sentence."

Concepts About Print

- Where to begin writing or reading, going from left to right

- Where to go after the end of the line (return sweep)

- Concept of a letter, word, sentence

- Concept of first and last part (of the word, sentence, story)

- Letter order in words is important

- There are first and last letters in words

- Upper and lower case letters have purpose

- Different punctuation marks have meaning

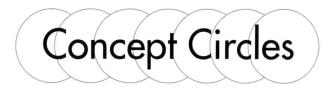

Concept Circles

This vocabulary strategy helps students determine conceptual similarities in words to help identify concepts. Three different tasks are associated with Concept Circles. To prepare Concept Circles, first identify the concept you want the students to learn and identify, then determine other words that either fall within that concept or describe that concept. Concept circles cannot be used to identify character traits or personality traits of people.

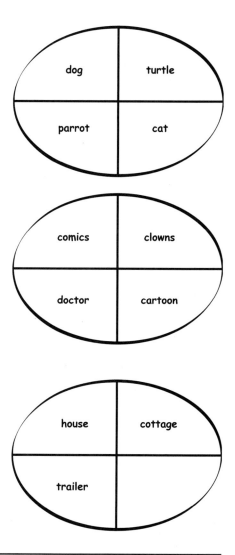

Task One

> What do all the words in the circle have in common? Name the category/concept on the line.

_____

Task Two

> Which word in the circle doesn't belong? Shade the space with the word that doesn't belong. Name the category/concept that the other words represent.

_____

Task Three

> What do the three words in the circle have in common? Add another word that is similar to the other three. Name the concept/category.

_____

From "Drawing Concept Circles: A New Way to Teach and Test Students" by James H. Wandersee, from _Science Activities_, Vol. 24, No. 4, Nov/Dec 1987, pp. 9–20. Reprinted with permission of the Helen Dwight Reid Educational Foundation. Published by Heldref Publications, 1319 Eighteenth St., NW, Washington, DC 20036-1802. Copyright © 1987.

Dolch Words

Dolch Words

As students master new concepts, they need to learn the Dolch words by sight. Edward W. Dolch developed this list of service words with pronouns, adjectives, adverbs, prepositions, conjunctions, and verbs. This list includes over 50 to 75% of the most commonly used words. The Dolch words are listed on the following page.

From *Problems in Reading* by Edward William Dolch, Champaign, IL: The Garrard Press, 1948.

Aa Bb Cc Tips for English Language Learners

- High-frequency words are abstract and difficult for many children to learn. Use plenty of oral language activities with these words. Children will use high-frequency words when they speak, even if the utterance is incomplete. Use children's language to create phrase cards and illustrations to help children expand their reading vocabularies.

José <u>and</u> Mike

Chandy <u>runs</u>.

Cal <u>is</u> small.

- Label objects in the classroom using high-frequency words and a noun. For example, the door to the classroom can be labeled "the brown door." Use a similar approach with other objects: a big clock, the white wall, our library, the teacher's desk, our reading corner, and so on. Link these phrases to ongoing lessons when appropriate.

Dolch Words

List 1	List 2	List 3	List 4	List 5
Preschool	Kindergarten	First Grade	Second Grade	Third Grade
a	an	after	always	about
and	are	again	around	better
away	at	an	because	bring
big	ate	any	been	carry
blue	be	as	before	cleat
can	black	ask	best	cut
come	brown	by	both	done
down	but	could	buy	draw
find	did	every	cat	drink
for	do	fly	cold	eight
funny	eat	from	does	fail
go	four	give	don't	far
help	get	going	fast	full
here	good	had	first	got
in	have	has	five	grow
is	he	her	found	hold
it	into	him	gave	hot
jump	like	his	goes	hurt
little	new	how	green	if
look	no	last	its	keep
make	now	know	made	kind
me	on	let	many	laugh
my	our	live	off	light
not	out	may	or	long
one	please	of	pull	much
play	pretty	old	read	myself
red	ran	once	right	never
run	ride	open	sing	only
said	say	over	sit	own
see	she	put	sleep	pick
the	so	round	tell	seven
three	soon	some	their	shall
to	that	stop	these	show
two	there	take	those	six
up	they	thank	upon	small
we	this	them	us	start
where	too	then	use	ten
yellow	want	think	very	today
you	was	walk	wash	together
	well	were	which	try
	went	when	why	warm
	what		wish	
	white		work	
	who		would	
	win		write	
	with		your	

Drawing Conclusions

Draw a picture of your conclusions from the story. Then write a sentence about your picture.

Elkonin Boxes—
Phonemic Awareness
Segmentation Activity

Elkonin Boxes— Phonemic Awareness Segmentation Activity

c	a	t

d	e	s	k

f	i	sh

Families of Words or Rimes

Children enjoy songs based on nursery rhymes, and these nursery rhymes contain frequently used rimes, or word families. These rhymes help them discover the words created by combining an onset of one or more consonant letters with a rime.

Rime	Nursery Rhyme Title
-ack	"I Saw a Ship A-Sailing"
-an	"Ladybug, Ladybug, Fly Away Home"
-at	"Jack Sprat Could Eat No Fat"
-ate	"One, Two, Three, Four"
-aw	"See-Saw, Margery Daw"
-ay	"Georgie Porgie"
	"Hickety, Pickety, My Black Hen"
	"Rain, Rain, Go Away"
-eat	Tom, Tom, the Piper's Son
-ell	"Peter, Peter, Pumpkin-Eater"
-ice	"An Apple Pie, When It Looks Nice"
-ick	"Jack Be Nimble"
-ide	"If Wishes Were Horses"
-ight	"Star Light, Star Bright"
-ill	"Jack and Jill"
-in	"Crosspatch, Draw the Latch"
-ing	"Sing a Song of Sixpence"
	"Sing, Sing, What Shall I Sing?"
	"Yankee Doodle"
-ink	"If All the World Were Paper"
-it	"There Once Were Two Cats of Kilkenny"
-ock	"Hickory Dickory Dock"
-oke	"There Was an Owl"
-op	"Higglety, Pigglety, Pop!"
-ore	"The Queen of Hearts"

"Webbing into Literacy" created by Dr. Laura B. Smolkin, Curry School of Education, University of Virginia, Charlottesville, VA 22904-4273, http://curry.edschool.virginia.edu/go/wil. Used by permission.

Families of Words

A phonogram, or rime, is a spelling pattern or word family. From these 37 most frequently used patterns a child can master 500 primary words (Wylie and Durrell, 1970).

Rime	Words Formed by Combining an Onset and a Rime
-ack	back, knack, lack, pack, rack, sack, snack, tack
-ail	bail, fail, hail, mail, nail, pail, rail, sail, snail, tail, trail
-ain	brain, chain, drain, gain, grain, lain, main, pain, train
-ake	bake, cake, brake, fake, flake, rake, sake, shake, take
-ale	bale, dale, gale, male, pale, sale, tale, scale, stale, whale
-ame	blame, came, fame, frame, game, lame, name, same, tame
-an	bran, can, man, fan, pan, plan, ran, scan, tan, than, van
-ank	bank, blank, clank, plank, prank, sank, tank, thank
-ap	cap, gap, lap, map, nap, rap, sap, snap, strap, tap, trap
-ash	brash, cash, crash, dash, flash, mash, sash, smash, trash
-at	bat, brat, cat, chat, fat, flat, hat, rat, sat, spat, mat, pat, that
-ate	date, fate, gate, grate, late, mate, plate, rate, skate, state
-aw	caw, claw, draw, gnaw, jaw, law, paw, raw, saw, straw
-ay	bay, bray, clay, day, hay, jay, lay, may, play, ray, say
-eat	beat, cheat, feat, heat, meat, neat, pleat, seat, treat, wheat
-ell	bell, cell, dell, dwell, sell, smell, spell, tell, well, yell

Reference: Wylie, Richard E., & Durrell, Donald D. (1970). Teaching vowels through phonograms. *Elementary English, 47,* 787–791.

-est	best, blest, crest, guest, jest, nest, rest, test, vest, west, zest
-ice	dice, mice, nice, slice, spice, splice, rice, thrice, twice
-ick	brick, chick, kick, lick, pick, quick, sick, slick, tick, trick
-ide	bride, glide, hide, pride, ride, side, slide, stride, tide, wide
-ight	bright, fight, fright, knight, light, might, night, right, sight
-ill	bill, drill, fill, grill, hill, pill, sill, skill, spill, still, thrill, will
-in	chin, fin, grin, kin, pin, skin, sin, spin, tin, thin, win, twin
-ine	dine, fine, line, mine, nine, pine, shine, spine, vine, whine
-ing	cling, fling, king, sing, sling, spring, ring, thing, wing, zing
-ink	blink, drink, link, mink, pink, rink, shrink, sink, think, wink
-ip	dip, drip, flip, grip, hip, rip, ship, sip, tip, trip, whip, zip
-it	bit, hit, fit, flit, kit, knit, lit, pit, quit, skit, sit, split, wit
-ock	block, clock, dock, flock, knock, lock, rock, sock, stock
-oke	broke, choke, joke, poke, smoke, spoke, stroke, woke, yoke
-op	chop, cop, crop, drop, flop, mop, pop, shop, stop, top
-ore	core, chore, more, pore, score, snore, sore, store, tore, wore
-ot	blot, clot, cot, dot, got, knot, lot, not, plot, rot, spot, tot, trot
-uck	buck, cluck, duck, luck, pluck, snuck, struck, tuck, truck
-ug	bug, dug, drug, hug, jug, mug, rug, shrug, slug, snug, tug
-ump	bump, dump, hump, lump, plump, pump, slump, stump
-unk	bunk, chunk, dunk, hunk, junk, slunk, spunk, sunk, trunk

Four-Square Vocabulary

This strategy helps students develop personal understandings for key vocabulary words and concepts (Johns & Lenski, 2005). Students fill out a grid that contains key information about the word. To be effective, this strategy should focus on no more than two or three key vocabulary words.

DIRECTIONS

1. Draw a sample Four-Square Vocabulary grid on the chalkboard or overhead transparency to model the process for students. Select a word they will already know. For example, if you use the word *happy*, their Four-Square Vocabulary grid might look like this.

Word	Makes me think of . . .
Happy	Playing with friends, birthday parties, and cartoons
Meaning	Opposite
Glad	Sad

2. Have children fold a sheet of paper in half in length and then in width to form four boxes. Have them label each of the boxes using the words *Word, Makes me think of . . . , Meaning,* and *Opposite.* If you prefer, you can give children grids that already contain the labels. Be sure children understand the meanings of the words used for labels.

3. Give the children key words from the unit they are studying. It is important to select words they have already encountered in their reading, discussion, and activities.

4. Have children fill out the Four-Square Vocabulary grids.

5. Provide time for children to share their grids with their peers. Discuss how and why children may have made different personal associations as part of their grids. Discuss the importance of "making new words on their own" by connecting them to their life experiences.

Four-Square Vocabulary

Name _____ Date _____

Word	Makes me think of . . .
Meaning	**Opposite**

Word	Makes me think of . . .
Meaning	**Opposite**

FAVORITE BOOK SHOW AND TELL

Since literacy is a social process, children benefit from meaningful opportunities to share and discuss books with their peers. The Favorite Book Show and Tell strategy allows children to share their favorite books as well as to learn about books their classmates enjoy. This strategy also supports the children's listening and speaking skills.

DIRECTIONS

1. Inform children that you will be having Favorite Book Show and Tell time each day. Explain to the children that each of them will have a chance to share a favorite book with the class. Clarify that the books can come from the children's homes, the public library, the school library, or the classroom library. Explain that the books can be new to the class or ones that have been read and shared together. Allow children to repeat a book if it is a favorite for more than one child in the classroom. Also, explain that children can select books that have been read to them or books they have read on their own.

2. Model the Favorite Book Show and Tell process using a book the children know from the classroom. Show the book to the children and say something such as, "The book *Lily's Purple Plastic Purse* is written by Kevin Henkes (1996). It is one of my favorites because it is funny, and Lily is an interesting character. I also like the pictures because they have some funny surprises hidden in them. The book has a happy ending, and it teaches a lesson too. I would recommend this book to anyone who likes funny books and stories about school."

From Laurie Elish-Piper, Jerry L. Johns, and Susan Davis Lenski, *Teaching Reading Pre-K–Grade 3,* Third Edition. Copyright © 2006 by Kendall/Hunt Publishing Company. Reprinted with permission.

Glass Analysis

Expose one word on a card, and make sure the student is always looking at the card. The whole word is always presented. Parts of a word are never covered up for identification.

Questionnaire Technique:

A. Using the word /song/

This word says /song/.
What does the word say?

In the word /song/,　　　　　　what letter makes the /s/ sound?
　　　　　　　　　　　　　　what letters make the /ong/ sound?
　　　　　　　　　　　　　　what letters make the /song/ sound?

In the word "song,"　　　　　what sound does the letter s̲ make?
　　　　　　　　　　　　　　what sound do the letters o̲ n̲ g̲ make?
　　　　　　　　　　　　　　what sound do the letters s̲ o̲ n̲ g̲ make?

What does the word say?

B. Using the word /stronger/

This word says /stronger/.
In the word stronger,　　　　what letters make the /str/ sound?
　　　　　　　　　　　　　　what letters make the /ong/ sound?
　　　　　　　　　　　　　　what letters make the /strong/ sound?
　　　　　　　　　　　　　　what letters make the /er/ sound?
　　　　　　　　　　　　　　what letters make the /onger/ sound?
　　　　　　　　　　　　　　what letters make the /stronger/ sound?

In the word stronger,　　　　what sound do the letters s̲ t̲ r̲ make?
　　　　　　　　　　　　　　what sound do the letters o̲ n̲ g̲ make?
　　　　　　　　　　　　　　what sound do the letters s̲ t̲ r̲ o̲ n̲ g̲ make?
　　　　　　　　　　　　　　what sound do the letters e̲ r̲ make?
　　　　　　　　　　　　　　what sound do the letters o̲ n̲ g̲ e̲ r̲ make?
　　　　　　　　　　　　　　what sound do the letters s̲ t̲ r̲ o̲ n̲ g̲ e̲ r̲ make?

What does the word say?

Optional:
If I take off /strong/, what sound is left?
If I take off the /er/ sound, what would be left?

From "Teaching Decoding as Separate from Reading" by Gerald G. Glass, Adelphi University Press, as appeared on /www.glassanalysis.com. Reprinted by permission of ETL, Inc.

Graphic Organizers for Thematic Units

KWL Chart—a graphic organizer that indicates what students <u>K</u>now, <u>W</u>ant to know, and <u>L</u>earn (Ogle, 1986, 1989).

Semantic Feature Analysis Chart—this chart or grid helps students to examine related concepts and make distinctions among them according to particular criteria used to compare their characteristics. This helps students to condense and organize data.

	Mammals	Reptiles	Amphibians
Dogs	+	−	−
Cats	+	−	−
Frogs	−	−	+
Hamsters	+	−	−
Turtles	−	+	−

Story Map—a graphic organizer that helps students to identify story grammar and create their own stories. The components of a story map can be used to help students predict events in a story and form connections with story elements.

Triarama—a three-dimensional, triangular display that is often made of construction paper. This display can be used to illustrate stories or help students to remember key concepts from the stories they read.

Venn Diagram—a graphic organizer with overlapping circles that show those features either unique or common to two or more concepts. Students might use Venn Diagrams to compare their own **language experience stories**, which they dictate to a teacher, with the stories they read in books.

Hidden Word

In the Hidden Word strategy, specific words are deleted from a text to focus the children's attention on using context to figure out what word makes sense in each blank. The teacher selects one or more words to cover in a passage and guides the children to predict what word(s) would make sense in the passage by using the context.

DIRECTIONS

1. Select a passage and copy it onto an overhead transparency. You may need to enlarge the passage so children can easily see it.

2. Identify two or three words to teach in the passage. When selecting the words to teach, be sure there are sufficient context clues to help the children figure out the missing words. Cover the target words using "sticky notes" or masking tape.

3. Display the transparency and tell the children you will be working together to figure out what words would make sense in the blanks.

4. Read the passage aloud with the children. Discuss the gist of the passage to ensure that children have grasped the major ideas.

5. Point out that some of the words have been covered. Then tell the children that you will be using the context to make predictions about what words could fit into the blanks.

6. Ask the children to predict what words would make sense in the first blank. As they share predictions, ask them to explain how they used the context to come up with their ideas.

7. After several children have shared and supported their predictions, pull the "sticky note" or masking tape off to reveal the actual word in the passage. Discuss the actual word in comparison to the children's predictions.

8. Follow steps 6 and 7 until all of the blanks in the passage have been discussed.

Hinky Pinks

Phonics Activity for Spelling Patterns/Rhyming/Rime Patterns

Examples: A large hog: is a _____ig _____ig
              A plane in the rain: is a w_____ j_____
              An unhappy boy: is a _____ad _____ad
              A chubby feline: is a f____ c____

From the book *Old Black Fly* by Jim Aylesworth, illustrated by Stephen Gammell

A naughty boy: a ____ad ____ad
A book bag: a ____ack ____ack
A big bouncy tummy: a ___elly ___elly
A dessert crumb: a ____ake ____ake

High-Frequency Words

OVERVIEW	The purpose of this assessment is to ascertain the child's ability to automatically identify a sample of the most common words in English. The words on the Revised Dolch List occur frequently in all types of printed materials. If you want to assess children's knowledge of these basic words, use one of the forms provided. The words selected for these assessments are the 50 most frequently used words in English. You could also make your own assessments by selecting other words from the Revised Dolch List if children know the basic words in these assessments. How children perform on the assessments will inform you about what words you may want to target for instruction to the entire class, small groups, or individual children.
MATERIALS NEEDED	1. Child's copy, either Form 1 (page 40) or Form 2 (page 42) 2. A copy of the Record Sheet that corresponds to the form selected for use, either Form 1 (page 41) or Form 2 (page 43) 3. Two blank sheets of paper
PROCEDURES	1. Duplicate the Record Sheet corresponding to the form selected for use. 2. Choose one form of the assessment. Cover the words with the two sheets of paper so only one word will be uncovered at a time. Place the page containing the covered words before the child. Say, "I want you to say some words for me. Let's begin with this one." 3. Move one of the blank sheets of paper below the first word and ask the child to say the word. If the child says the number, cover it up and point to the word. As the child says words, note correct responses with a plus (+) in the appropriate place on the Record Sheet. Record any incorrect responses by using the following markings (or your own system).

Marking	Meaning of Marking	Marking	Meaning of Marking
man men	Substitution	m— men	Partial Pronunciation
		<u>men</u>	Repeated word
man s/c men	Self-correction	small ∧men	Insertion
~~men~~	Omitted word	the/small	Pause

---

4. Encourage the child to say "pass" or "skip it" for any unknown words. Say, "Just do the best you can." Stop the assessment if no response is given to the first four words.
5. Proceed through the words until the assessment is completed. If you observe anxiety, frustration, or reluctance on the part of the child, use your professional judgment to determine if the assessment should be stopped.

SCORING AND INTERPRETATION

Count the number of words pronounced correctly and record the score in the box on the Record Sheet. Self-corrections are counted as correct, but make a note about any words that were not known automatically. The intent of this assessment is to determine if the child knows the most common words in English at sight. Mispronunciations, partial words, refusals, saying "don't know," and self-corrections are evidence that the words are not known automatically. These words may become the basis for instruction using the teaching strategies described in Section 4.1. The same form of the assessment could be used after targeted instruction to note gains in basic sight word knowledge. Form 2 of the assessment could be used after the child had near mastery of the words on Form 1 or as a further assessment of the child's knowledge of the most common words in English.

1. the
2. and
3. a
4. is
5. it
6. for
7. he
8. as
9. they
10. be
11. at
12. from
13. I

14. have
15. but
16. were
17. all
18. when
19. their
20. her
21. we
22. about
23. said
24. if
25. would

Form 1—High-Frequency Words—Child's Copy

RECORD SHEET

Form 1

High-Frequency Words

Name _____ Date _____

Teacher's Directions   38–39
Child Copy   40

BRIEF DIRECTIONS

Present one word at a time for the child to pronounce. Say, "I want you to say some words for me. Let's begin with this one." Use a plus (+) for correct responses. Record the child's responses for incorrect words. Total correct responses and put the score in the box.

1. the _____

2. and _____

3. a _____

4. is _____

5. it _____

6. for _____

7. he _____

8. as _____

9. they _____

10. be _____

11. at _____

12. from _____

13. I _____

14. have _____

15. but _____

16. were _____

17. all _____

18. when _____

19. their _____

20. her _____

21. we _____

22. about _____

23. said _____

24. if _____

25. would _____

Total Correct ☐

1. of

2. to

3. in

4. that

5. was

6. you

7. on

8. are

9. with

10. his

11. or

12. had

13. not

14. this

15. by

16. one

17. she

18. an

19. there

20. can

21. what

22. up

23. out

24. some

25. so

RECORD SHEET

Form 2

High-Frequency Words

Name _____ Date _____

Teacher's Directions   38–39
Child Copy   42

BRIEF DIRECTIONS

Present one word at a time for the child to pronounce. Say, "I want you to say some words for me. Let's begin with this one." Use a plus (+) for correct responses. Record the child's responses for incorrect words. Total correct responses and put the score in the box.

1. of _____

2. to _____

3. in _____

4. that _____

5. was _____

6. you _____

7. on _____

8. are _____

9. with _____

10. his _____

11. or _____

12. had _____

13. not _____

14. this _____

15. by _____

16. one _____

17. she _____

18. an _____

19. there _____

20. can _____

21. what _____

22. up _____

23. out _____

24. some _____

25. so _____

Total Correct [   ]

Homophone
Picture Cards

See

I <u>see</u> things with
my eyes.

Sea

The boat was sailing
on the vast <u>sea</u>.

44

Ice Cream Man Phonics Activity

The Ice Cream Man*

The ice cream man rings his bell.
He has some frozen treats to sell.
Chocolate or cherry,
or even strawberry,
they look as good as they smell.

—Karen McGuigan Brothers

Word Bank Words: The Ice Cream Man

bell	sell	smell
man	treats	cream
swell	ran	dream

Ways to sort (categories):

1. /ell/, **2.** /e/, **3.** /an/, **4.** words that contain a consonant blend, **5.** words that refer to things that can be eaten, **6.** words with two of the same letters (e.g., sell, treats)

Cloze Sentences

1. Ice cream is one of my favorite_____.

2. I_____all the way home from school today.

3. My dad thinks that sweet treats are_____.

4. Our trip to Disney World is a _____come true.

5. I love the _____of cookies in the oven.

Write a short story using the words from the word bank.

*"The Ice Cream Man" by Karen McGuigan Brothers, and excerpts from Timothy Rasinski and Belinda S. Zimmerman, *Phonics Poetry: Teaching Word Families, 1/e.* Published by Allyn and Bacon, Boston, MA. Copyright © 2001 by Pearson Education. Reprinted by permission of the publisher and Karen McGuigan Brothers.

? Interview Questions ? for Tutoring ?

The following diagnostic questions are designed to identify the needs and interests of children. These questions will make it easier to establish goals and choose reading strategies for effective tutoring.

1. Tell me how you feel about reading.

2. What do you like to read?

3. Are there certain books or authors you like most?

4. What are your favorite books?

5. Do you like to go to the library? Do you have books of your own?

6. Describe your reading class in school?

7. What does your teacher do during reading class?

8. What do you do when you have trouble understanding what you read?

9. What do you like to do during your spare time? What is your favorite thing to do?

10. Are there particular books you would like to read during our time together?

Jack's Lunch Phonics Activity

Jack's Lunch*

Jack likes to pack
his lunch in a sack.
He's very well fed
On jelly and bread
With cookies for a snack.

—Karen McGuigan Brothers

Word Bank Words: Jack's Lunch

pack	snack	sack
jelly	lunch	well
belly	munch	sells

Ways to sort (categories):

1. /   /   **2.** /   /   **3.** /   /   **4.** words that refer to _____,
5. words that begin with_____, **6.** words with_____syllables

Cloze Sentences

1.

2.

3.

4.

5.

Other Activities

1. Do a survey of favorite lunch foods. Display the results as a set of bar graphs.

2.

---

*"Jack's Lunch" by Karen McGuigan Brothers, and excerpts from Timothy Rasinski and Belinda S. Zimmerman, *Phonics Poetry: Teaching Word Families, 1/e.* Published by Allyn and Bacon, Boxton, MA. Copyright © 2001 by Pearson Education. Reprinted by permission of the publisher and Karen McGuigan Brothers.

Journal for Connections with Stories

Word or Quote	Thought or Connection

K-W-L Chart

K-W-L (Ogle, 1986) is intended to help students activate background knowledge prior to reading an informational selection or beginning a unit of study. The *K* invites students to share or list what they *know* about a topic before they read or begin a unit of study. The *W* identifies *what* students want to find out, and the *L* indicates what students *learned* from the reading material or unit of study. A chart (see below) is typically used with the strategy.

DIRECTIONS

1. Present children with a K-W-L chart on the chalkboard or provide an individual copy of the chart for each student. Young children can participate orally while the teacher writes ideas. Older children can write their own ideas individually or in small groups. The teacher should then develop a master chart.

K—What We Know	W—What We Want to Find Out	L—What We Learned and Still Need to Learn

Categories of Information:

2. Explain the chart to children. For the first few times the strategy is used, children may profit from participating as a whole group with the teacher recording their ideas. The goal of the *K* is to invite children to brainstorm what they think they know about the topic. Incorrect statements should also be listed; they will be evaluated in light of the reading selection or unit of study. It is also possible for children to suggest categories of information they hope to find out during the reading or unit of study. For example, if the topic is whales, some possible categories are types and sizes, where they live, and what they eat. Model as needed and guide children in developing appropriate categories. You might ask children about enemies of whales if they do not suggest that category.

3. Have children then suggest some questions that they want to have answered. Write these questions in the *W* column. Capitalize on children's interests and any uncertainties that may be evident from the initial brainstorming. The goal should be to move students to the point that they generate their own questions; however, do not expect this outcome in the initial use of K-W-L.

4. After children have read the selection, they should write down what they have learned, what they still want to find out, and any initial information that was revealed to be incorrect as a result of the reading. Further reading and research may help children find answers to those questions that were unanswered.

5. Variations of K-W-L can include mapping ideas from what was learned (e.g., different types of whales; what whales eat) and preparing a written summary of their learning.

Keys for Technology Reviews

ABCs of Technology

<u>A</u>pplication—How does this website relate to learning standards and skills?

<u>B</u>enefits—What are the benefits of this website? What literacy strategies and skills are addressed on this website? Is the design of this website appealing?

<u>C</u>ontent—Describe the content of this website. Do you have any concerns?

Literature for Literacy Stations

Elkonin Boxes

Fox, M. (1993). *Time for bed.* New York: Scholastic.
Fox, M. (2004). *Where is the green sheep?* New York: Harcourt, Inc.

Hinky Pinks

Keats, E. J. (1971) *Over in the meadow.* New York: Scholastic.
Marshall, J. (1991). *Old Mother Hubbard and her wonderful dog.* New York: Scholastic.

Making Words

Keats, E. J. (1977). *Whistle for Willie.* New York: Puffin Books.
Shannon, D. (2000). *The rain came down.* New York: Scholastic.

Rounding Up the Rhymes

Aylesworth, J. (1994). *My son John.* New York: Henry Holt and Company.
Aylesworth, J. (2003). *Naughty little monkeys.* New York: Dutton Children's Books.

Secret Message

Brown, M. (1985). *Hand rhymes.* New York: Puffin Unicorn Books.
Lewis, P. (1998). *The House of Boo.* New York: Atheneum Books for Young Readers.

Word Building

Carle, E. (1993). *Today is Monday.* New York: Scholastic.
Ehlert, L. (2001). *Waiting for wings.* New York: Harcourt, Inc.

Word Sorts

Martin, B., & Sampson, M. (2001). *Little granny quarterback.* Honesdale, Pennsylvania: Caroline House.

Letter Chart for
Individual Word Walls

A	B	C	D
E	F	G	H
I	J	K	L
M	N	O	P
Q	R	S	T
U	V	W	X
Y	Z		

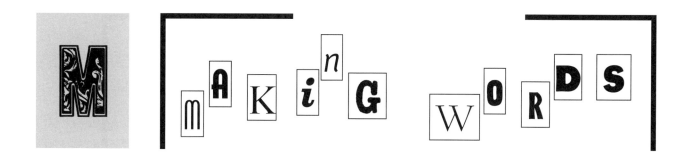

Making Words is a hands-on phonics strategy that helps children see patterns in words as they manipulate letter cards or tiles (Cunningham & Hall, 1998). This strategy helps children understand letter and sound associations as they work with word families or onsets and rimes. An onset is the beginning part of a word that comes before the vowel. For example, in the word *cat*, the onset is *c*. A rime is the part of the word from the vowel to the end. For example, in the word *cat*, the rime is *at*. Rimes are sometimes referred to as phonograms, spelling patterns, or word families. In the Making Words strategy, children manipulate letter cards or tiles to build words that start out small and get longer as the lesson progresses. Typically, a Making Words lesson focuses on one or more rimes or spelling patterns that the children are learning. Refer to Appendix B on the CD-ROM for a list of rimes or word families. For lists of words and sample lessons for the Making Words strategy, consult Cunningham & Hall (1998).

DIRECTIONS

1. Choose the word that will be the longest word made in the lesson (e.g., splash).
2. Make a list of other words that can be made using the letters in the word *splash*. Arrange these words to show how changing letter order or adding a new letter can form a new word. An example follows.

    a   Al   as   has   ash   lash   splash

3. Select the words you will include in your lesson. Consider the patterns and words that can be made by rearranging letters in a previous word. Proper nouns can be included to help children learn about using capital letters correctly.
4. Make letter cards on large index cards for each letter needed for the lesson. Write each consonant in black and each vowel in red. Write each word for the lesson on a small index card. Place the large letter cards in a pocket chart.
5. Make individual letter cards for each child. This can be done by writing letters on index cards or small squares of paper. Letter tiles can also be used.
6. Distribute a set of letters to each child. Provide a few minutes for the children to explore the letters and words they can make with their letter cards.
7. Say, "Use two letters to make the word *as*. I am *as* tall *as* Bill." Remind the children that each word must have a vowel (red letter).
8. Pause for a moment while the children make the word with their letter cards. Ask for a volunteer to come to the front of the class and make the word using the large letter cards in the pocket chart. Provide time for the children to self-check the words they made.
9. Say, "Add one letter and make the word *has*. He *has* a pet dog."
10. Ask for a volunteer to make the word in the pocket chart. Have children self-check their own words.
11. Continue the lesson using the same steps with the other words.
12. When you have used all of the words on your list except the last word (splash), challenge the children by saying, "See what word you can make using all of your letters."

Mapping Words

Pictorial Word Web

Mapping Words

Semantic Word Map

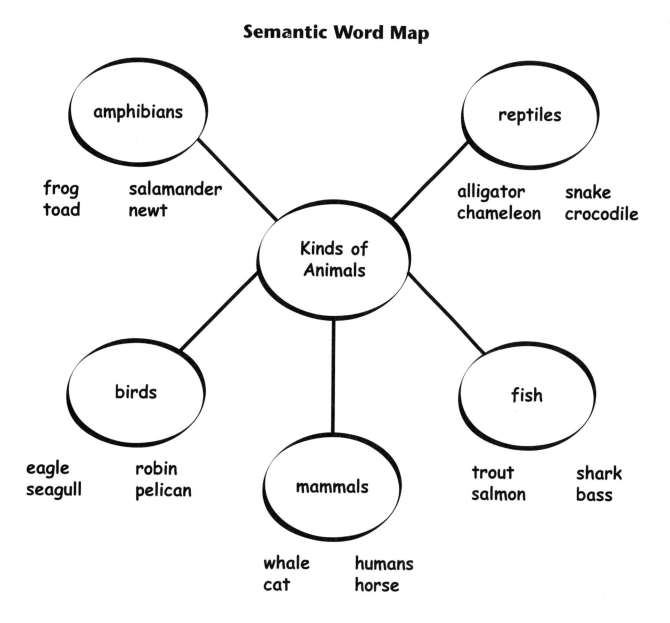

amphibians

reptiles

frog
toad

salamander
newt

alligator
chameleon

snake
crocodile

Kinds of
Animals

birds

fish

eagle
seagull

robin
pelican

mammals

trout
salmon

shark
bass

whale
cat

humans
horse

Frog and Toad Character Map

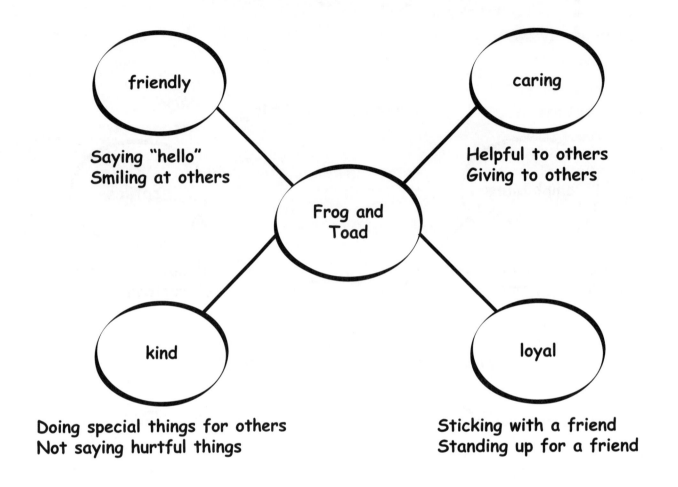

friendly

Saying "hello"
Smiling at others

caring

Helpful to others
Giving to others

Frog and
Toad

kind

Doing special things for others
Not saying hurtful things

loyal

Sticking with a friend
Standing up for a friend

This mapping activity coordinates with Arnold Lobel's book *Frog and Toad Are Friends,* which was published by Harper-Festival in 1990.

Mystery of the Stuffed Animal

Linking Language

This activity provides a hands-on opportunity to integrate language arts and science. As children solve the mystery, they use descriptive language as visual clues are eliminated. One child describes a mystery item to another child who cannot see it. The child who is guessing will need to pose questions to get more information about the mystery item. This helps children to identify animal characteristics and learn to ask effective questions to identify animals that have been described.

Objectives

- Students will identify the characteristics of stuffed animals.
- Students will describe those characteristics to a group of children.
- Children will guess the identity of those animals using the clues that are given.

Vocabulary Words to Introduce:

- mystery
- sack
- guess
- clue
- think
- soft
- big
- little
- small
- large

Materials

- stuffed animals (children could bring them from home)
- pillowcase
- box (large enough to cover mystery items)

Procedure

- One child fills a pillowcase with familiar stuffed animals.
- She tells the other children to close their eyes or to face in the opposite direction.
- She takes an animal from the pillowcase and hides it from view under a box.
- She tells the other children to open their eyes or to turn around.
- She uses words to describe the mystery animal without naming it.
- The other children listen as descriptions are given.
- Then they ask questions that will help to identify the stuffed animal.
- After the stuffed animal is identified, another child takes a turn selecting an animal and describing it to the other children.

"Mystery of the Stuffed Animal" from *Linking Language: Simple Language and the Literacy Activities Throughout the Curriculum,* p. 20 (ISBN 978-0-87659-202-7) by Robert Rockwell, Debra Reichert, and Bill Searcy. Reprinted with permission from Gryphon House, P.O. Box 207, Beltsville, MD, 20704-0207. (800) 638-0928. www.ghbooks.com.

Closure

- Discuss what students noticed about the stuffed animals.
- Discuss the clues that made it easiest to discover the identity of the stuffed animals.
- Help children to realize the power of adjectives during this discussion.

Extensions

- Describe characteristics of specific categories of animals.
- Coordinate ideas from this lesson with semantic maps that show features of animals.
- Children could do concept sorts with animal figurines and discuss their characteristics.

Questions for Assessment of Language Development

- Expressive Language—Can children give enough information to allow a reasonable guess?
- Receptive Language—Do children listen for descriptive words that enhance their guessing?

Literacy Connections

Reading Experiences

- *Golden Bear* by Ruth Young
  Children will enjoy this rhythmic story about a little boy and his perfect companion, a golden bear.
- *Jamaica's Find* by Juanita Havill
  Jamaica finds a cuddly toy dog in the park, and she takes it home. Later, Jamaica finds the girl who belongs to the dog and makes a new friend.
- *Just Look* by Tana Hoban
  Peep through the hole and try to guess what object is in the brilliant photos. Then turn the page to see if you are right.
- *Where's My Teddy?* by Jez Alborough
  When Eddie loses his teddy bear and tries to find it in the woods, he meets a very large bear with the same problem.

Writing Experiences

- Language Experience Approach—Make a class chart of the children's stuffed animals. Let children dictate a sentence about their stuffed animals. Record their words on the chart. (Examples might include: "Tim brought a yellow dog." or "Miranda brought a shiny, green snake.") Read the chart together, pointing to the words as you read. Leave it up for several days to read again and again.
- Have small blank books available for children to create books about their own stuffed animals. Pages can be used to describe their animals. For example, "My teddy bear is brown. My teddy bear is fuzzy." Encourage them to write, or write their words for them in their books.
- Help children make riddle charts. On large paper children will write or dictate a clue describing one of the stuffed animals. On the back they will illustrate and write the answer. Hang up the charts and read them together.

  http://www.literacyconnections.com/LAStuffedAnimalMystery.php

  Robert Rockwell, Debra Reichert Hoge, and Bill Searcy show kid-friendly ways for the practice of oral language skills.

Narrative Retelling

OVERVIEW	You can get a good sense of children's knowledge of story structures by their story retelling. Children who have a developed sense of story will be able to retell stories using story grammar, but those who are unclear about story structure will tell unrelated details. Children's retelling of stories can let you know whether they need more instruction in story structure.
MATERIALS NEEDED	1. An age-appropriate story that is new to the child 2. A copy of the Narrative Retelling Record Sheet on page 60
PROCEDURES	1. Choose a short book that is new for the child. The book should have an obvious plot with named characters. You may choose to use props or puppets with the story if you think visual aids could help the child. 2. Before reading the book say, "I'm going to read a story to you. After I am finished reading, I will ask you to tell me the story as if you were telling it to someone who has not read the story. As you listen, try to remember as much of the story as you can." 3. Read the book aloud to the child. 4. After you have read the book say, "Now tell me as much of the story as you can." If the child hesitates, ask probing questions such as "What was the story about?" or "Who was in the story?" or "What happened next?" You may want to tape-record the retelling for future reference.
SCORING AND INTERPRETATION	Use the Narrative Retelling Record Sheet to record how well the child understands narrative story structure and the rubric for a score. If a child scores below a 4, you should continue to teach story structure explicitly. Have the child participate in another retelling within a short time for a second assessment. Some stories are easier for a child to retell than others, and a second retelling may provide different information.

Narrative Retelling

Name _____ Date _____

Name of text _____

CHECK ALL THAT APPLY

_____ Identifies setting of story.

_____ Identifies main characters.

_____ Identifies problem of story.

_____ Identifies sequence of events.

_____ Identifies solution to problem.

RUBRIC FOR NARRATIVE TEXT RETELLING

4   Child correctly retells story using the setting, names of characters, events as they occurred in the story, the problem, and the solution. Events are described thoroughly and events are in correct sequence.

3   Child correctly identifies setting and some of the characters although without exact names, tells the events in sequence, identifies the story's problem and solution. There are some errors in retelling, but most details are accurate.

2   Child identifies the setting and characters and gives some information about the plot. Details may be minimal.

1   Child identifies few story elements correctly.

Opening Doors by Teaching How Words Work

There are 12 different ways we can "play" with words in the English language. All of these ways listed below can be used to help children learn how flexible words are and to manipulate parts of words. You can use magnetic letters on boards, cut-out letters, whiteboards with markers, or felt letters on felt board to help children physically manipulate words. Make it a game, inviting students to add, delete, and change word parts so they become flexible in taking apart and constructing words. **Word Building** is a good activity that uses many of these principles.

Principles for Teaching How Words Work

• You can add letters to the beginning of a word to make a new word (*h + and = hand*).
• You can add letters to the end of a word to make a new word (*sea + t = seat*).
• You can change the first letter of a word to make a new word (*car, tar*).
• You can change the last letter of a word to make a new word (*had, has*).
• You can use a word you know to solve a new word (*car, cart; part, party*).
• You can add endings to make new words (*book, books; read, reading*).
• You can change the beginning and ending letters of a word to make new words (*his, hit, sit*).
• You can change the middle letter or letters to make new words (*cat, cut; chair, cheer*).
• You can add letters or letter clusters to make new words (*it, pit; pitch, pitcher*).
• You can use parts of words you know to figure out words you don't know (*tree + play = tray; she + make = shake*).
• You can show that some words sound the same and look different (*sail, sale*).
• You can show that some words look the same and sound different (*present, present*).

Observation Form for Classroom Visits

Name _____ Date _____

Child's name _____ Grade _____

Location of observation: _____ Time: _____ to _____

Purpose of observation:

Predictions about what you'll see:

Significant events during observation:

Reflective analysis of significant events: (What did you learn?)

How can you use what you observed in your tutoring sessions?

Teacher's Signature _____ Date _____

Phoneme Spelling Chart

Phonemes, Spellings, Example Words, and Meaningful Names

PHONEME	SPELLING(S) AND EXAMPLE WORDS	MEANINGFUL NAMES
/A/	a (table), a_e (bake), ai (train), ay (say)	Long A; Fonzie's greeting
/a/	a (flat)	Crying baby; baby lamb; home alone
/b/	b (ball)	Beating heart; drum
/k/	c (cake), k (key), ck (back)	Nutcracker; golf shot; camera
/d/	d (door)	Knocking; dribbling ball
/E/	e (me), ee (feet), ea (leap), y (baby)	Long E; shriek
/e/	e (pet), ea (head)	Rocking chair; creaky door; hard of hearing
/f/	f (fix), ph (phone)	Angry cat; clothes brush; electric fan; soda fizz
/g/	g (gas)	Croaking frog, gulping soda
/h/	h (hot)	Out of breath; warm breath; tired dog
/I/	i (I), i_e (bite), igh (light), y (sky)	Long I
/i/	i (sit)	Crying puppy; icky sticky; baby pig
/j/	j (jet), dge (edge), g[e, i, y] (gem)	Scrub brush; wood rasp; jump rope
/l/	l (lamp)	Flying saucer; mixer
/m/	m (my)	Mmm mmm good; delicious sound
/n/	n (no), kn (knock)	Mosquito; motorboat
/O/	o (okay), o_e (bone), oa (soap), ow (low)	Long O; Oh, I see
/o/	o (hot)	Say ah; doctor sound; cool drink; yawn
/p/	p (pie)	Popcorn; water drip; stone skip; soap bubbles
/kw/	qu (quick)	Coffee pot; typewriter
/r/	r (road), wr (wrong), er (her), ir (sir), ur (fur)	Chain saw; angry lion; robot; growling dog

From http://www.auburn.edu. Reprinted by permission of Bruce Murray, Auburn University.

PHONEME	SPELLING(S) AND EXAMPLE WORDS	MEANINGFUL NAMES
/s/	s (say), c[e, i, y] (cent)	Flat tire; hair spray; sizzling bacon
/t/	t (time)	Ticking clock; timer; automatic sprinkler
/U/	u (future), u_e (use), ew (few)	Long U
/u/	u (thumb), a (about), e (loaded), o (wagon)	I dunno; mother bear; punch in the stomach; foghorn
/v/	v (voice)	Electric shaver; airplane; vacuum
/w/	w (wash)	Lariat; fly rod; washing machine
/ks/ or /gz/	x (box, exam)	Soda can; grease gun
/y/	y (yes)	Sticky mess
/z/	z (zoo), s (nose)	Buzzing bee; arc welder; zipper
/OO/	oo (boot), u (truth), u_e (rude), ew (chew)	Ghost; howling wolf; owl
/oo/	oo (book), u (put)	Lifting weights; chin-up bar
/oi/	oi (soil), oy (toy)	Seal; squeaky gate; spring
/ou/	ou (out), ow (cow)	It hurts; inoculation; sting
/aw/	aw (saw), au (caught), a[l] (tall)	Poor thing; crow
/ar/	ar (car)	Spinning tire; grinding gears; gargle
/sh/	sh (ship), ti (nation), ci (special)	Be quiet; watering the lawn
/hw/	wh (white)	Blow out the candle
/ch/	ch (chest), tch (catch)	Old train; antique car; chipmunk
/th/ or /th/	th (thick, this)	Peeling tape; angry goose; wet shoes
/ng/	ng (sing), n (think)	Gong; string bass
/zh/	s (measure)	Sawing wood; sander

Questions and Predictions Chart

Question	Prediction

Quick Story Planning Chart

Title: _____

Beginning	Middle	End			

Recognizing Rhyme Assessment

Phoneme Awareness Assessment Tool

Directions

I am going to say two words: **cat – sat.**
I want you to tell me if the two words sound alike. This is called a rhyme.
Let me show you.

Model

Cat and **sat** have the same sound at the end so they rhyme. **Cat** and **mop** do not rhyme because the do not have the same sound at the end.

Share

Listen to these two words: **pail – tail.**
Now say the two words with me: **pail – tail.**
Do these two words rhyme? **(Yes)**
Put your thumbs up like this if they rhyme:

Listen to these two words: **cow – pig.**
Now say the two words with me: **cow – pig.**
Do these two words rhyme? **(No)**
Put your thumbs down like this if they do not rhyme:

Assess

Listen to these sets of words. Thumbs up if they rhyme. Thumbs down if they do not rhyme. Here we go . . .

1. *fin – win*

2. *rug – mug*

3. *hat – dress*

4. *pan – man*

5. *bird – book*

6. *lock – rock*

7. *bet – get*

8. *cup – dog*

Recognizing Rhyme Assessment: Phoneme Awareness Assessment Tool designed by Dr. Adria Klein from http://teams.lacoe.edu. Reprinted by permission of Adria F. Klein, Ph.D.

Rhyme Detection

OVERVIEW	This assessment will help determine the child's ability to hear whether or not words rhyme. This skill is helpful in learning phonics. It is also often taught early in phonemic awareness instruction. Form 1 may be used as a pretest early in the school year. Form 2 may be used later in the year or after specific instruction in rhyming.
MATERIALS NEEDED	1. A copy of the Record Sheet for Form 1 (page 69) or Form 2 (page 70).
PROCEDURES	1. Practice saying the words on the list. 2. Say the following to the child, "I want you to tell me if two words rhyme. When words sound the same at the end, they rhyme. *Hat* rhymes with *cat*. Does *look* rhyme with *book?* Yes. Does *mat* rhyme with *bat?* Yes. But not all words rhyme. *Mice* does not rhyme with *soon* because *mice* ends with *ice* and *soon* ends with *oon*. Does *cat* rhyme with *pig?* No. Does *sick* rhyme with *pick!* Yes. Now, listen carefully. I'm going to say some words, and I want you to tell me if they rhyme." 3. Say all the words distinctly but in a normal voice. 4. Place a ✓ in the appropriate column to indicate whether the child's response was correct or incorrect.
SCORING AND INTERPRETATION	Count the number of correct items and record the total on the appropriate Record Sheet on page 69 or page 70. Informally judge the child's ability to detect rhymes. If the child could profit from additional instruction in rhyme detection, refer to the instructional strategies and activities in Section 3.2.

Additional Ways of Assessing Rhyme

1. Many poems and nursery rhymes provide an informal opportunity to assess the child's ability to rhyme. Note the child's ability to predict a rhyming word at the end of a line of a poem or rhyme.

2. Listen to children's language play in the classroom and on the playground. Watch for evidence of rhyming as children play a variety of games (e.g., jump rope).

From Laurie Elish-Piper, Jerry L. Johns, and Susan Davis Lenski, *Teaching Reading Pre-K–Grade 3,* Third Edition.

RECORD SHEET

Form 1

Rhyme Detection

Teacher's Directions   68
Child's Copy   None

BRIEF DIRECTIONS

Say to the child: "I want you to tell me if two words rhyme. When words sound the same at the end, they rhyme. *Hat* rhymes with *cat*. Does *look* rhyme with *book?* Yes. Does *mat* rhyme with *bat?* Yes. But not all words rhyme. *Mice* does not rhyme with *soon* because *mice* ends with *ice* and *soon* ends with *oon*. Does *cat* rhyme with *pig?* No. Does *sick* rhyme with *pick?* Yes. Now, listen carefully. I'm going to say some words, and I want you to tell me if they rhyme." Place a ✓ in the appropriate column, total correct responses, and record the score in the box.

			Correct	Incorrect
1. bee	—	see	_____	_____
2. tall	—	call	_____	_____
3. jet	—	dog	_____	_____
4. can	—	man	_____	_____
5. him	—	gym	_____	_____
6. hen	—	bag	_____	_____
7. rat	—	sat	_____	_____
8. room	—	zoom	_____	_____
9. back	—	sing	_____	_____
10. bake	—	rake	_____	_____

Total Correct ☐

Observations, Comments, Notes, and Insights

From Laurie Elish-Piper, Jerry L. Johns, and Susan Davis Lenski, *Teaching Reading Pre-K–Grade 3,* Third Edition. Copyright © 2006 by Kendall/Hunt Publishing Company. Reprinted with permission.

RECORD SHEET

Form 2

Rhyme Detection

Teacher's Directions   68
Child's Copy   None

BRIEF DIRECTIONS

Say to the child: "I want you to tell me if two words rhyme. When words sound the same at the end, they rhyme. *Hat* rhymes with *cat*. Does *look* rhyme with *book?* Yes. Does *mat* rhyme with *bat?* Yes. But not all words rhyme. *Mice* does not rhyme with *soon* because *mice* ends with *ice* and *soon* ends with *oon*. Does *cat* rhyme with *pig?* No. Does *sick* rhyme with *pick?* Yes. Now, listen carefully. I'm going to say some words, and I want you to tell me if they rhyme." Place a ✓ in the appropriate column, total correct responses, and record the score in the box.

			Correct	**Incorrect**
1. me	—	he	_____	_____
2. ball	—	mall	_____	_____
3. hog	—	let	_____	_____
4. than	—	ran	_____	_____
5. skim	—	trim	_____	_____
6. rag	—	men	_____	_____
7. that	—	fat	_____	_____
8. green	—	broom	_____	_____
9. ring	—	sack	_____	_____
10. shake	—	bake	_____	_____

Total Correct ☐

Observations, Comments, Notes, and Insights

Responding to Plot

Children can respond to stories in a number of ways when they react to the plot of the story (Moss, 1995). They can respond to the characters, the events in the story, and the problem. When children respond to the plot, they can even make connections to their own lives.

DIRECTIONS

1. Select a book to read to children or that children can read independently that has a clear plot and interesting characters. The plot should have an identifiable problem, events in a sequence, and a resolution to the problem. Characters can be humans or animals, but they should be developed so that children can form an opinion.

2. Explain to children that they will be responding to the plot or the characters in the story after reading.

3. Read the book aloud or have children read independently.

4. Duplicate and distribute the response questions on page 83. Read the questions with children, explaining terms as needed.

5. Tell children that they should select one question to answer as a response to the story. Emphasize that no response is incorrect but that responses reflect individual ideas. Provide children with adequate time for writing.

6. After children have finished writing their responses, invite them to share their responses with their peers.

7. Encourage children to write responses using the Response Questions when they read on their own.

Aa Bb Cc Tips for English Language Learners

- In order for children to respond to text, they need to have some background knowledge about the topic or some connection to parts of the story. Children who do not speak English may have similar backgrounds to the English speakers in your classroom, or they may have very different experiences. Au (2000) reminds us that, as educators, we need to connect instruction to children's experiences rather than connecting children to instruction. Therefore, as you select books for children's responses, choose books that have themes that are familiar to all children.

Response Questions

1. Who was your favorite character? Why?

2. Was there a character you did not like? Why?

3. What was your favorite part of the story? Why?

4. Who was the hero or heroine? How do you know?

5. Who was the villain? How do you know?

6. Was there a helper? What did this character do?

7. What was the problem in the story? How was it solved?

8. What do you think is the most important thing to remember about this story?

9. Does this story remind you of any other story you have read or heard?

10. What did you think of the illustrations? Did you find anything in the pictures that was not included in the words?

Adapted from Moss, J.F. (1995). Preparing focus units with literature: Crafty foxes and authors' craft. In N.L. Roser & M.G. Martinez (Eds.), *Book talk and beyond: Children and teachers respond to literature* (pp.53–65). Newark, DE: International Reading Association.

From Laurie Elish-Piper, Jerry L. Johns, and Susan Davis Lenski, *Teaching Reading Pre-K–Grade 3,* Third Edition. Copyright © 2006 by Kendall/Hunt Publishing Company. Reprinted with permission.

Story Map

Title _____

Author _____

Setting	Characters
Problem	
Event 1	
Event 2	
Conclusion	

Story Frame

A Story Frame is a summary outline of an entire story. After reading a story, children can fill in the blanks of a Story Frame to improve their comprehension (Fowler, 1982). You can create a general Story Frame as in the example below or write one specifically for a story or passage.

DIRECTIONS

1. Identify a story or a passage that has a plot that children can easily identify. Read the story aloud or have the children read it independently or with partners.

2. Encourage children to construct meaning from the story by reminding them to use comprehension monitoring strategies. Remind them to use fix-up strategies if they lose track of the story's plot.

3. After the children have finished reading, remind them of the elements of the story. Explain that every story has a problem but that the problem might be something the main character wants done. For example, the problem in the story *Rainy Day Fun* (Palazzo, 1988) is that the children are trying to think of what they could do on a rainy day. Explain that this is the problem of the story and that events will happen through the story to solve the problem. Have children identify the solution to the problem. In *Rainy Day Fun* (Palazzo, 1988), the children decided to put on a play.

4. After children have identified the problem in the story, remind them that stories are told by events in sequential order. Have them identify the events in the story they have read.

5. Ask children to retell the story they read. Remind them to state the problem of the story, the events in the plot, and how the problem was solved. If they forget any part of the plot, direct the children to reread that portion of the story.

6. Provide children with a copy of a Story Frame. Tell them that they should fill in the blanks so that the entire paragraph tells part of the story. Children can work with a partner or independently.

7. Identify one of the children's Story Frames that correctly tells the story. Read it aloud to the children. Have children check their Story Frames to determine if they understood the story. A copy of a Story Frame is on the following page.

Story Frame

Name _____ Story Title _____

In this story, the problem starts when _____

_____

After that, _____

_____

Next, _____

_____

Then, _____

_____

The problem is finally solved when _____

_____

The story ends _____

_____

Shared Reading

Shared Reading replicates the bedtime story sharing situation with an individual, a small group, or a classroom of children. This strategy allows children to participate in and enjoy books they cannot read on their own (Mooney, 1990). The emphasis of this strategy is on enjoyment of the story as a whole. Teachers can introduce a wide range of exciting books to children through Shared Reading.

DIRECTIONS

1. Select a children's book with predictable text and engaging illustrations. If you are reading with a large group of children, a Big Book will work well.

2. Have children sit so they all can hear the story and see the illustrations. A story rug is a helpful addition to the classroom.

3. Show the children the cover of the book and read the title. Ask them to make predictions about the contents of the book. Invite selected children to respond to some of the ideas that are shared.

4. Read the story aloud, inviting children to read along if they would like to do so.

5. Provide time for the children to share their personal responses and favorite parts of the book.

6. Reread the book, inviting the children to read along if they would like to do so.

7. Place the book in the classroom library so the children can read it during their free time.

Aa Bb Cc Tips for English Language Learners

- Select predictable books with clear illustrations to provide clues for English Language Learners during shared reading. An extensive listing of predictable books can be found in Johns and Lenski (2005).

- Provide time for English Language Learners to engage in a picture walk to see the story before starting the shared reading. The picture walk allows children to look at the pictures and think about what the story line might be before hearing the actual story. To do a picture walk, have the children look at the cover and discuss what they see. Progress through the book, directing the children's attention to pictures that convey important information about the story. Direct helpful questions to the children. After viewing and discussing the pictures, begin reading the story with the children.

Shared Reading
Lesson Plan

1. Title of Lesson and Grade Level(s)

   Present a book in a creative way, and clearly describe what you will say as you initially present the book. Demonstrate your awareness of both students and content through your selection and innovative presentation of these elements.

2. Objective(s) and Standards Addressed

   Design objectives that demonstrate your ability to plan meaningful instruction based on appropriately selected content and curriculum goals.

3. Materials

   Identify a variety of teaching materials, including technology, to enhance student learning during this lesson.

4. Procedures, Including Motivation, Body of the Lesson, and Closure

   Discuss the procedure for your lesson in specific ways. Show your ability to integrate a thorough understanding of students, the subject matter being taught, and the curriculum. Provide evidence of your understanding of the cognitive processes involved in various types of learning. Describe ways you will give students opportunities to participate in the lesson and share reading opportunities. Indicate ways you will include learning communities with interpersonal and small-group communications.

5. Accommodations for Diverse Students

   Describe specific instructional opportunities for students with widely diverse developmental and learning needs.

6. Assessment

   Discuss the specific ways you will use formal and informal assessments that are linked to lesson objectives to promote learning.

Secret Messages

Take words the children know and use them as the basis for new words that will be formed by removing the onsets and replacing them with new onsets. Once the new onsets have replaced the old onsets of the words, the newly formed words will create a "secret" message formed by putting the words together in the order they come in the sequence. See examples below:

Take **H** from **He** and put in **W.**   **(We)**
Take **b** from **bike** and put in **l.**   **(like)**
Take **d** from **do** and put in **t.**   **(to)**
Take **l** from **late** and put in **sk.**   **(skate)**

Secret message: We like to skate.

Take **D** from **Dive** and put in **F.**   (   )
Take **f** from **filly** and put in **s.**   (   )
Take **b** from **bats** and put in **c.**   (   )
Take **str** from **stray** and put in **pl.**   (   )
Take **f** from **fat** and put in **c.**   (   )
Take **bl** from **bland** and leave the rest.   (   )
Take **h** from **house** and put in **m.**   (   )

Secret Message: Five silly cats play cat and mouse.

Tutorial Planning

Tutor _____Date_____Session _____

Objectives

Book(s)

Strategies

Reflections

Future Plans

Tutorial Log Sheet

Tutor_____

Child's "name" _____Grade____Date_____Time: _____to_____(Total_____)

ACTIVITY/STRATEGY/SKILL done w/tutee	TEACHER REFLECTION (Tell how the session went, what you would do differently, and why.)
READING STORY (comp. skill, asking ?s, discussing, literary element)	
DECODING/PHONICS (word recog., sight wds./hi-freq wds., ABC order)	
VOCABULARY (word **meanings**, not word recog.) **List specific words.**	
WRITING (tutee's personal response, creative writing, story summary)	
WHAT WILL YOU DO NEXT TIME AND WHY?	

Three-Minute Conferences

OVERVIEW	Select up to 10 words that the children have been taught and provide a list to the children. When you meet with each child for the Three-Minute Conference, ask the child to use each word in a meaningful way. By meeting with three children per day, you should be able to meet with all of the children in the class over approximately a two-week period.
MATERIALS NEEDED	1. A pencil or pen 2. Record Sheet on page 82
PROCEDURES	1. Tell the children you will be holding Three-Minute Conferences to assess their knowledge of vocabulary words they have recently studied. Provide the list to the children. 2. Begin holding the Three-Minute Conferences the next day. 3. Say one of the vocabulary words and ask the child to use it in a meaningful way (give a sentence, explain meaning in own words, or give a clear example). 4. Record the child's performance. 5. Continue through the remaining words on the list.
SCORING AND INTERPRETATION	Evaluate the child's performance by checking the appropriate column on the record sheet: C = complete and indicates that the child understands the word fully and can use it in a meaningful manner; P = partial and indicates that the child has some knowledge of the word but does not have a full understanding; and N = no, the child does not have meaningful knowledge related to the word.

RECORD SHEET

Three-Minute Conferences

Name _____ Date _____

WORD	NOTES ON CHILD'S PERFORMANCE	KNOWLEDGE OF WORD C = complete P = partial N = no

Unlocking Doors with Children's Books

Children's Books with Specific Short Vowel Sounds

Short a

Baker, K. (1999). *Sometimes.* New York: Harcourt Brace.

Cameron, A. (1994). *The cat sat on a mat.* Boston: Houghton Mifflin.

Flanagan, A. K. (2000). *Cats: The sound of short a.* Elgin, IL: The Child's World.

Griffith, H. (1982). *Alex and the cat.* New York: Greenwillow.

Kent, J. (1970). *The fat cat.* New York: Scholastic.

Most, B. (1980). *There's an ant in Anthony.* New York: Morrow.

Short e

Ets, M. H. (1972). *Elephant in a well.* Bergenfield, NJ: Viking.

Flanagan, A. K. (2000). *Ben's pens: The sound of short e.* Elgin, IL: The Child's World.

Galdone, P. (1973). *The little red hen.* New York: Scholastic.

Lionni, L. (1994). *An extraordinary egg.* New York: Knopf.

Short i

Lankford, M. D. (1991). *Is it dark? Is it light?* New York: Knopf.

Leonard, M. (1998). *Get the ball, Slim.* Brookfield, CT: Millbrook.

McPhair, D. (1984). *Fix-it.* Bergenfield, NJ: Viking.

Sanfield, S. (1995). *Bit by bit.* East Rutherford, NJ: Viking.

Short o

Anholt, C., & Anholt, L. (1992). *All about you.* Bergenfield, NJ: Viking.

Flanagan, A. K. (2000). *Hot pot: The sound of short o.* Elgin, IL: The Child's World.

Freeman, D. (1955). *Mop top.* Bergenfield, NJ: Viking.

Hutchins, P. (1968). *Rosie's Walk.* New York: Simon & Shuster.

Seuss, D. (1965). *Fox in socks.* New York: Random House.

Short u

Marshall, J. (1984). *The cut-ups.* Bergenfield, NJ: Viking.

Seuss, D. (1982). *Hunches and bunches.* New York: Random House.

Udry, J. M. (1981). *Thump and plunk.* New York: Harper & Row.

Children's Books with Specific Long Vowel Sounds

Long a

Aardema, V. (1981). *Bringing the rain to Kapiti Plain.* New York: Dial.

Flanagan, A. K. (2000). *Play day: The sound of long a.* Elgin, IL: The Child's World.

Henkes, K. (1987). *Sheila Rae, the brave.* New York: Greenwillow.

Munsch, R. (1987). *Moira's birthday.* Buffalo, NY: Firefly.

Long e

Chardiet, B., & Maccarone, G. (1992). *We scream for ice-cream.* New York: Scholastic.

Cowley, J. (1994). *The screaming mean machine.* New York: Scholastic.

Keller, H. (1983). *Ten sleepy sheep.* New York: Greenwillow.

Long i

Cameron, J. (1979). *If mice could fly.* Riverside, NJ: Atheneum.

Gelman, R. (1979). *Why can't I fly?* New York: Scholastic.

Gordh, B. (1999). *Hop right on.* New York: Golden Books.

Minarik, E. E. (1978). *No fighting! No biting.* New York: Harper Collins.

Long o

Buller, J., & Schade. S. (1992). *Toad on the road.* New York: Random House.

Johnston, T. (1972). *The adventures of Mole and Troll.* East Rutherford, NJ: Viking.

Wild, M. (1994). *Going home.* New York: Scholastic.

Long u

Lobel, A. (1966). *The troll music.* New York: Harper & Row.

Segal, L. (1977). *Tell me a Trudy.* New York: Farrar, Straus & Giroux.

Slobodkin, L. (1959). *Excuse me—certainly!* New York: Vanguard Press.

Vocabulary Venn Diagram

Some very simple words in our language have more than one meaning. A vocabulary Venn diagram is a useful and simple way to show children these multiple meaning words.

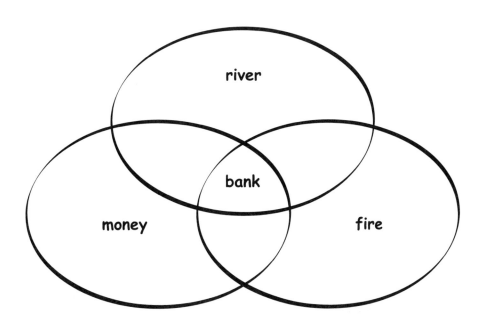

Vocabulary Pictures

Draw pictures or glue pictures to depict understanding of the meaning of vocabulary words. A student writes each word at the top and a short definition for the word. Below the picture, the student writes a sentence that goes along with what is happening in the picture or drawing. For example . . .

mast

a tall pole that holds up the sail on a sailboat

Mast

The strong wind bent the masts that held up the sails!

mansion

a very large house with many rooms where rich people live

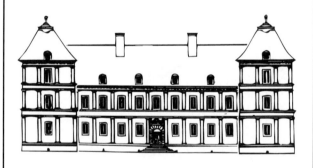

Bill Gates lives in a mansion because he is very rich.

Word BUILDING

The goal of word building is to change the beginning, middle, and end of each word enough to ensure that the child has to pay attention to the different parts of the word before he/she determines what the word is. If a teacher just changed the onset, the child would only pay attention to the beginning of the word because he/she would potentially already know the rime of the word. The teacher must carefully plan the sequence of the task using the given letters in order to ensure that the child is practicing the onsets, rimes, and middle vowel patterns of words that present challenges for the child during decoding.

Use the following letters to create a sequence in which you change up the beginnings, endings, and middles of words throughout the sequence. Try to end with the same word you started with in the sequence. For example:

a, c, r, t, f, i, x, g, n

car

Change the '**c**,' to a '**t**', and now we have '**tar**.'

I can change the '**r**' to a '**g**,' and now I have '**tag**.'

I can change the '**g**' to an '**x**,' and now I have '**tax**.'

I can change the '**t**' to an '**f**,' and now we have '**fax**.'

I can change the '**a**' to an '**i**,' and now we have '**fix**.'

I can change the '**x**' to an '**n**,' and now I have '**fin**.'

I can change the '**f**' to a '**t**,' and now I have '**tin**.'

I can change the '**i**' to an '**a**,' and now I have '**tan**.'

I can change the '**n**' to a '**g**,' and now we have '**tag**.'

I can change the '**g**' to an '**r**,' and now we have '**tar**.'

I can change the '**t**' to a '**c**', and now we have '**car**'.

car

Word Map and Word Riddles

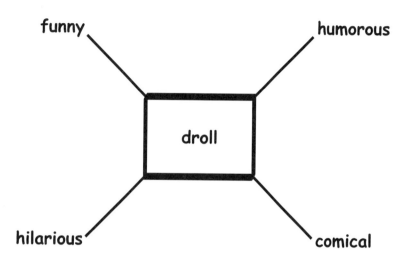

funny   humorous

droll

hilarious   comical

Young children are very interested in jokes, riddles, and puns. These types of word play contribute to children's interest in words. The development of vocabulary riddles "is a way to stimulate exploration of words and to build interest and flexibility in word learning" (Blachowicz, 1998, p. 10).

DIRECTIONS

1. Share several riddles with the children. For example, you might share some of these old favorites.

   What is black and white and read all over? A newspaper!

   How did the sick pig get to the hospital? He took a hambulance!

   What do you call a duck that gets all A's in school? A wise quacker!

2. Explain to the children that you can write your own word riddles by following a few simple steps (Thaler, 1988). First, choose a subject for the riddle. For example, you might select *plant* because the children have been studying this topic in science.

3. Tell the children you will take the word *plant* and remove the first part to leave you with *ant.*

4. You will then make a list of words that begin with *ant.* Your list might include

   antonym   antenna   anticipate

5. Explain to the children that you will then add back the missing letters *pl* and make up riddles for the words. The riddles you create might include

   What is the opposite of a plant? A plantonym!

   How does a tree feel where it's going? It uses its plantenna!

   How does a tree know what is going to happen next? It can planticipate things!

6. Provide time for the children to write and share other word riddles.

Word Sorts

The human brain is a pattern detector that seeks to categorize or sort information to make it more meaningful. Such categorizing or sorting "allows us to find order and similarities among various objects, events, ideas, and words that we encounter" (Bear, Invernizzi, Templeton, & Johnston, 2004, p. 61). The word sorting strategy allows students to engage in this process as they search, compare, and contrast words to identify meaningful patterns and generalizations about letters and sounds.

DIRECTIONS

1. Determine the purpose of your word sorting activity. Is it to focus the children's attention on sounds, or do you want to target patterns such as word families? This lesson will focus on a sound sort for beginning sounds.

2. Prepare picture cards for the words you want the children to sort. You can create these cards yourself or you may wish to use the pictures provided in the book *Words Their Way* (Bear, Invernizzi, Templeton, & Johnston, 2004). Also prepare a letter card for each beginning sound students will sort for in the activity. For example, if you are targeting the letters *b* and *c* you would prepare a letter card for each as well as approximately 6–8 picture cards for each letter. For the letters *b* and *c* you could include the pictures:

    b - ball, boy, bat, box, bed, bug, bell, bus

    c - cat, cow, cup, coat, corn, can, car, cake

3. Explain to the children that they will be looking at pictures, saying the word the picture represents, and figuring out the beginning sound for the word. Model the process by saying the following.

    This is a picture of a ball. *Ball* begins with /b/.

4. Tell the children that you will put the picture of the ball under the letter *b* because *ball* begins with /b/.

5. Continue with several more cards to ensure the children understand the process.

6. Provide a set of letter cards and picture cards for children to sort the words at their desks or in small groups.

7. Word sorts can be adapted to match various phonics instructional goals. Some examples of other types of word sorts are listed in the box below.

WORD SORTS

Picture sorts for beginning blends (e.g., bl, cl, sp, dr)	Picture sorts for long vowels
Picture sorts for beginning digraphs (i.e., wh, ch, sh, th)	Word sorts for CVC words
Picture sorts for beginning short vowels	Word sorts for CVCe words
Picture sorts for medial short vowels	Word sorts for r-controlled vowels
	Word sorts for hard and soft *c* or *g*

Word Wall

The Word Wall strategy is helpful for teaching high-frequency words. The words are taught to children, and then they are posted on the Word Wall for future reference. A variety of hands-on activities are also incorporated into Word Wall instruction to help children learn and remember the high-frequency words (Cunningham, 2000). Typically, teachers will spend a few minutes each day teaching and reviewing new Word Wall words over the course of a week. The following directions provide suggestions for teaching Word Wall words over a period of several days.

DIRECTIONS

1. Select up to five target high-frequency words to teach in a week. Word lists containing high-frequency words, children's spelling errors, and grade-level curricula are sources of words for the Word Wall.

2. Introduce each word to students by writing it on an index card and using the word in a sentence. Write the sentence on the chalkboard and underline the Word Wall word.

3. Ask children to suggest other sentences that use the Word Wall word. Discuss the meaning or use of the word.

4. Point to each letter of the word as you spell it aloud. Invite children to spell the word with you as you point to each letter.

5. Trace around the configuration of the word using another color of chalk. Discuss the shape of the word.

6. Follow this pattern for each of the new Word Wall words. Place the index cards for the five new words on the Word Wall. Arrange the words alphabetically and use a different color of index card or ink for each new word.

7. Engage children in the Clap, Chant, and Write activity. Ask children to number a piece of scratch paper from one to five. Say each word, using it in a sentence. Ask children to write each word on their paper. Then have children clap and chant the spelling of each word as you lead the process. Have children correct their own spellings.

8. On another day, select five words appropriate for rhyming. Ask children to review rhymes using the Word Wall. Have children number a sheet of scratch paper from one to five. Ask them to write a Word Wall word that rhymes with the word you give to them. Give children the rhyming word and the first letter as clues. For example, you might say the word begins with *m* and rhymes with *by*. Continue this pattern for all five Word Wall words.

9. Guide children to check their own words. Ask them to say the word they wrote and to spell it aloud when you call each number and restate the clues. For example, after you say, "Number 1. The word begins with /m/ and rhymes with *by*," children should respond, "My, m-y." Continue with this pattern until all five words have been checked. Ask children to correct their work as you complete this step.

10. On another day, engage children in a cross-checking activity with the Word Wall words. Tell the children that they will need to select the Word Wall word that makes sense in a sentence and begins with a certain letter. For example, tell the children, "The word begins with *t* and fits in the sentence I went to _____ store yesterday." Continue with this pattern with all five Word Wall words.

11. Have children check their own words by reading each sentence again and restating the beginning letter of the word. Ask children to chant the word and then the spelling for each of the five Word Wall words.

What's the Word?

When I come to a word I don't know . . .

✓ I look at the picture.

✓ I think about the story.

✓ I look at how the word begins.

✓ I get my mouth ready to say the word.

✓ I think about a word I know that has the same sound in it.

✓ I see what I know in the word.

✓ I try a word and see if it makes sense, sounds right, and looks right.

✓ I go back and try again.

Xylophones, Poems, and Songs for Learning

Poems, Songs, and Rhymes

A very natural and engaging way to help young children develop a favorable attitude toward reading is to capitalize on a wide variety of poems, songs, and nursery rhymes. It is possible to use these literary pieces to help develop sound awareness, speech-to-print matching, language flow, concepts for letters and words, and an understanding of print conventions (e.g., print goes from left to right and top to bottom in English). Some of the popular types of rhymes include lullabies ("Rock-a-bye Baby"), singing game rhymes ("Ring-a-Round O'Roses"), counting-out rhymes ("One, Two, Buckle My Shoe"), tongue twisters ("Peter Piper"), nonsense rhymes ("If All the World Were Paper"), and verse stories ("The Queen of Hearts"). They often appeal to children because of their sounds, rhymes, and strong rhythms.

DIRECTIONS

1. Consider the maturity and interest of children when selecting a poem, song, or rhyme. It should be fun for the children and have the potential to help achieve a a variety of teaching goals. For example, reciting "Jack and Jill" might be used to help children develop an understanding of rhyming.

2. Begin by sharing the selected material aloud. The children should listen. Read the material again and invite the children to join in as they are able. Read the material a third time in an echo reading fashion: read a line and have children echo it back to you. Then talk about the selection and invite children to share their ideas or reactions.

3. Present the material on a piece of chart paper or an overhead transparency. Read it while pointing to the words. Help the children understand that you are reading the words. Point out how the print flows and how the words rhyme. Carefully select the one or two aspects of language you wish to emphasize. Keep the sharing active and lively, stressing the joy and fun of the material.

4. Select additional material to share each day. Move gradually from oral sharing to reading the printed word. Some of the rhymes can be acted out ("One, Two, Buckle My Shoe") so take every opportunity to actively engage children.

5. As children begin memorizing the material, take opportunities to have them say the rhyme from memory at various times during the day. These words in memory can be used in later lessons to develop speech-to-print match and other print concepts. Songs may be particularly enjoyable to the children and help them make connections to print as they demonstrate their interest. Children can also be shown how to keep time with the rhyme by clapping their hands or rocking back and forth.

6. Write the various poems, songs, and rhymes on chart paper and post them around the room. Invite the children to read the materials independently, with partners, or in small groups.

7. One variation is to use dramatization with nursery rhymes (Roush, 2005). For "Little Boy Blue," get pictures, objects, or a video of the following: horn, sheep, meadow, corn, and haystack. Children can dramatize the rhyme by doing the following:

   Pretend to blow a horn; "baa" like a sheep; eat corn like a cow; put hands up as if questioning where Little Boy Blue is; pretend to be asleep.

Activities, tips, & Center Ideas

to Develop Rhyme

1. Read rhyming books or nursery rhymes to children every day. Reread many of the children's favorites several times. As children become familiar with specific rhymes, have them say the rhymes along with you as you read. From time to time, stop reading before the last word in a rhyming line and have children supply the rhyming word.

2. Call on children whose names have many rhyming words such as *Mike* and *Pam.* Say a word that rhymes with one of the names. Have children repeat the word along with the name that rhymes with it as in *Mike* and *spike* and *Pam* and *ram.*

3. Tell children that you are going to say three rhyming words. Say three words that rhyme such as *run, fun,* and *bun.* Tell children that you want them to listen carefully to the words and then think of more words that rhyme with the words that you said. For example, children could say the words *sun* and *spun.* If children make up a word, tell them that they need to think of words that everyone knows. Repeat this activity several times each week with different rhyming words.

4. Help children hear the difference between words that rhyme and words that do not rhyme. Say three words, two of which rhyme. For example, say *sail, mail,* and *made.* Have children say the three words with you. Then ask children which two words rhyme.

5. Sing or chant songs that contain rhyming words. Some songs that work well are *Five Little Monkeys, The Wheels on The Bus, The Name Game, A Hunting We Will Go, This Old Man,* and *The Ants Go Marching.* Sing or chant songs several times a day. After singing, point out some of the rhyming words.

6. Have a group of children act out their favorite nursery rhyme. Have the other children guess the name of the rhyme. Then have all of the children say the rhyme aloud.

7. Say a word that has many rhyming words such as *day.* Have children brainstorm words that rhyme with the original word such as *may, say, ray,* and *pay.* When possible, have children draw pictures of several of the words that rhyme with the original word.

8. Have children create silly rhyming names for characters in their favorite books or for their pets. For example, Clifford the Big Red Dog could be named Bifford. Encourage children to have fun with rhymes.

9. Have children sit in a circle. Say a rhyming word such as *spin.* Throw a soft ball to one of the children. The child who catches the ball should say a word that rhymes with *spin* such as *win.* That child should toss the ball to another child or back to you. The person who has the ball should think of another rhyme. Continue until no one can think of additional words that rhyme with the original word. Then begin with a new word.

10. Gather pairs of objects or pictures of objects whose names rhyme. Place the objects in a bag and have a child pick an object without looking. A second child also picks an object and decides if the names of the objects rhyme. If they rhyme, two new children are chosen. If the words do not rhyme, another child picks an object and decides if it rhymes with either of the words. Continue the process until all objects have been paired correctly.

11. Provide pictures and/or objects that rhyme and have children sort them into groups that rhyme. Begin, if possible, with actual objects.

12. Read a rhyming couplet and have children supply the missing word.

    If you are *bad,* mom will be _____ .

    If you see a *bee,* get me a cup of _____ .

    I saw a *rat;* you saw a _____ .

The Yopp–Singer Test of Phoneme Segmentation

Directions for administering the Yopp-Singer Test of Phoneme Segmentation

1. Have one test sheet for each student in the class that is to be assessed. **THIS TEST IS STRICTLY ORAL.** The child should not see the words on the list.

2. Assess students individually in a quiet place.

3. Keep the assessment playful and game-like.

4. Explain the game to the student exactly as the directions specify.

5. Model for the student what he or she needs to do with each of the practice words. Have them break apart each word with you.

Students are given the following directions upon administration of the test:

"Today we're going to play a word game. I'm going to say a word and I want you to break the word apart. You are going to say the word slowly, and then tell me each sound in the word in order. For example, if I say 'old': you should say '/o/-/l/-/d/.' (The teacher says the sound, not the letters.) Let's try a few words together."

The practice items are ride, go, and man. The teacher should help the student with each sample item, segmenting the item for the student if necessary and encouraging the student to repeat the segmented word. The student is then given the 22 item test. If the child responds correctly, the teacher says, "That's right." If the student gives an incorrect response, he or she is corrected. The teacher provides the appropriate response. The teacher circles the numbers of all correct answers.

The student's score is the number of items correctly segmented into all constituent phonemes. No partial credit is given. For instance, if a student says "/c/-/at/" instead of "/c/-/a/-/t/," the response may be noted on the blank line following the items but is considered incorrect for the purposes of scoring. Correct responses are only those that involve articulation of each phoneme in the target word.

Students who segment all or nearly all of the items correctly (17–22 items correct) may be considered phonemically aware. Students who correctly segment some items (7–16 correct) are displaying emerging phonemic awareness. Students who are able to segment only a few items or none at all (0–6 items correct) lack appropriate levels of phonemic awareness. Without intervention, those students scoring very low on this assessment are likely to experience difficulty with reading and spelling. These students should be provided with considerable linguistic stimulation that focuses on the sound structure of their spoken language in conjunction with their reading programs.

Yopp-Singer Test from Yopp, H. K. (1995, September). A test for assessing phonemic awareness in young children, *The Reading Teacher,* 49 (1), 20–29. Reprinted with permission of the International Reading Association.

Yopp–Singer Test of Phoneme Segmentation

Student's name _____ Date _____

Score (number correct) _____

Directions: Today we're going to play a word game. I'm going to say a word and I want you to break the word apart. You are going to tell me each sound in the word in order. For example, if I say "old," you should say "/o/-/l/-d/."

(Administrator: Be sure to say the sounds, not the letters, in the word.) Let's try a few together.

Practice items: (Assist the child in segmenting these items as necessary.) ride, go, man

Test items: (Circle those items that the student correctly segments; incorrect responses may be recorded on the blank line following the item.)

1. dog _____   12. lay _____

2. keep _____   13. race _____

3. fine _____   14. zoo _____

4. no _____   15. three _____

5. she _____   16. job _____

6. wave _____   17. in _____

7. grew _____   18. ice _____

8. that _____   19. at _____

9. red _____   20. top _____

10. me _____   21. by _____

11. sat _____   22. do _____

Yopp-Singer Test from Yopp, H. K. (1995, September). A test for assessing phonemic awareness in young children, *The Reading Teacher*, 49 (1), 20–29. Reprinted with permission of the International Reading Association.

Zipping Up the Learning with Terminology

Guide to Terms and Other Related Information

A. Some basics . . .

- **phoneme**—smallest unit of sound; there are 44 phonemes in English language and over 500 different spellings that represent these 44 phonemes! (**phonology** = the sounds in speech)

- **blending**—the ability to combine individual phonemes together so as to pronounce a meaningful word [example: /p/ + /i/ + /n/ =/pin/]

- **segmenting (segmentation)**—the process of separating spoken words or syllables into their individual phonemes [example: /spot/= /s/ + /p/ + /o/ + /t/]

- **phonemic awareness**—a basic understanding that speech is composed of a series of individual sounds (of spoken words). It is not reading letters, pronouncing letter names, or sounding out words! This is a great accomplishment for a child because phonemes are abstract language units that carry no meaning and they are not discrete units in speech because we often slur sounds together or clip them in speech. Some level of phonemic awareness is a prerequisite to learning to read!

- **grapheme**—written symbol used to represent the phoneme; can be one letter or more than one letter which combines to form one speech sound (phoneme); same grapheme can represent more than one phoneme [example: **gh** at beginning of word makes hard /g/ sound, but **gh** at end of word makes /f/ sound]

- **phonics**—the study of the relationships of letters in written words to the sounds they represent in spoken words; used for aiding decoding

- **decoding**—translating graphemes into the sounds of spoken language so as to pronounce a visually unfamiliar word [Educators refer to decoding as word identification and "sounding out the letters in words."]

- **morpheme**—smallest unit of meaning; prefixes, roots, and suffixes are morphemes because they carry meaning; **ing, ed, ies, es, s** are not suffixes; rather, they are inflectional endings that determine verb tense or number (plural). They do not carry meaning.

- **onset**—one or more consonant letters which come before the vowel phoneme in a syllable

- **rime**—the vowel and consonant letter(s) which come after the onset; There is only one vowel phoneme in a rime [ex: /oat/ after the onset /c/ is the rime; it only has one vowel sound, /o/]

- **syllable**—the unit of pronunciation; There can be only one vowel phoneme (sound) in a syllable; There are as many syllables in a word as there are vowel phonemes (sounds)

- **open syllable**—a syllable that ends in a vowel phoneme [play, blue, see]

- **closed syllable**—a syllable that ends in a consonant phoneme [truck, cheap]

- **diacritical mark**—marks that are added to a letter or symbol to show its pronunciation or to distinguish it in some way

- **breve**—a diacritical mark (˘) used to indicate the short or unglided sound of a vowel
- **macron**—a diacritical mark (ˉ) used to indicate a long or glided sound of a vowel
- **accent mark**—a dark slash that comes after the syllable pronounced the loudest in a word; If the word has 3 or more syllables, a light slash mark (secondary accent mark) comes after a syllable that is pronounced softer than the primary syllable
- **orthography**—the spelling patterns of written language

B. Some other terms and examples . . .

- **Digraph**—a grapheme compound of two letters that represent **one** speech sound (phoneme); there are **consonant digraphs** (see below) and **vowel digraphs** [examples: /ea/, /oa/, /ee/, /ie/, /ai/, /ou/, /oo/, /ei/, /ay/, /ey/]
- **consonant blend (cluster)**—a combination of two or more adjacent consonant phonemes pronounced rapidly and refers to the sounds in which the consonants represent; each consonant retains its sound; these are taught as units and not as separate phonemes, for example, /st/ is taught as /st/, not as /s/ + /t/.

  1. **examples of blends (clusters) found at the beginning and middle of words**
     /bl/, /cl/, /fl/, /gl/, /pl/, /br/, /cr/, /dr/, /fr/, /sc/, /sk/, sl/, /sm/, /sp/, /st/, /spl/, /squ/, str/, /tw/, /dw/
  2. **examples of blends (clusters) found at the end of words**
     /ld/, /lk/, /nd/, /nt/. /st/. sk/, /mp/, /ft/, /lt/

- **consonant digraph**—two letter consonant combinations that represent phonemes not represented by just a single letter; these two letter consonants combined make only one phoneme (sound)

Examples: /sh/ as in **sharp**; /ch/ as in **cheap**; /wh/ as in **white** /hw/, but not **wh** as in **who,** (the **wh** in who makes the phoneme /h/ as in **hat**; Also the voiced /th/ as in **this** and the voiceless /th/ as in **with;** Also, /ng/ only in the middle and ends of words, such as **gong, wing, sang, tongue, sung.**

- **diphthong**—a single vowel phoneme resembling a 'glide' from one sound to another represented by the graphemes **/oi/** as in **noise**, **/oy/** as in **toy**, **/ou/** as in **found**, and **/ow/** as in **cow**.
- **schwa**—a vowel phoneme found **only** in an unaccented syllable which represents a soft /uh/ sound and is indicated by the key symbol /ə/, which resembles an inverted 'e'; Each vowel can be pronounced as a schwa [examples: about, family, button, circus]
- **r-controlled vowels**—a vowel phoneme whose usual long or short sound is distorted because an 'r' follows it [examples: 'car', 'fir', 'her', 'short', 'spur', 'air', 'ear']

C. Key symbols used in Dictionary Pronunciation Keys

Because different dictionaries will have their own Pronunciation Keys and may use some key symbols that are different from the ones below, be sure to teach your students how to use the Pronunciation Key of the dictionaries you will use in your classroom.

/ă/ apple	/ā/ apron	/â/ care	/ir/ pier	/th/ thin
/ĕ/ elephant	/ē/ even	/ä/ father	/hw/ which	/zh/ azure
/i/ igloo	/ī/ icě	/ô/ ball, law	/ə/ about, item, edible, gallop, circus	
/ŏ/ ox	/ō/ open	/oo/ took	/ər/ butter	
/ŭ/ umbrella	/ū/ use	/oo/ boot	/th/ then	/ng/ ring

Zipping Up the Learning with Literature

Alphabet Books

A

A is for America by Devin Scillian
Alaska ABC Book by Charlene Kreeger
Alphabet Adventure by Audrey Wood
Alphabet City by Stephen T. Johnson
Alphabet Times Four-An International ABC by Ruth Brown
Alphabet Under Construction by Denise Fleming
America by Lynne Cheney
Animalia by Graeme Base
Animal Alphabet by Bert Kitchen
Animal Parade by Jakki Wood
Anno's Alphabet: An Adventure in Imagination by Mitsumasa Anno
Antics!: An Alphabetical Anthology by Catherine Hepworth
Appaloosa Zebra: A Horse Lover's Alphabet by Jessie Haas
Arctic Alphabet: Exploring the North from A to Z by Wayne Lynch
The ABC Mystery by Doug Cushman
The Alphabet Parade by Seymour Chwast
The Alphabet Tree by Leo Lionni
The Airplane Alphabet Book by Jerry Pallotta

B

B is for Bluegrass: A Kentucky Alphabet by Maryann McCabe Riehle
B is for Buckeye: An Ohio Alphabet by Marcia Schonberg
B is for Buckaroo: A Cowboy Alphabet by Louise Doak Whitney
Bugs A to Z (A+ Books) by Terri Degezelle
Butterfly Alphabet Book by Brian Cassie
The Bird Alphabet Book by Jerry Pallotta

C

C Is for Cornhusker: A Nebraska Alphabet by Rajean Luebs Shepherd
Canada from A to Z by Bobbie Kalman
Caribou Alphabet by Mary Beth Owens
Chicka Chicka Boom Boom by Bill Martin, Jr., John Archambault, and Lois Ehlert
City Seen From A To Z by Rachel Isadora
Clifford's ABC by Norman Bridwell
Caribbean Alphabet by Frane Lessac
Cowboy Alphabet by James Rice

D

D is for Democracy: A Citizen's Alphabet by Elissa Grodin
The Desert Alphabet Book by Jerry Pallotta
The Dinosaur Alphabet Book by Jerry Pallotta

E

Eating the Alphabet: Fruits and Vegetables from A to Z by Lois Ehlert
Elfabet by Jane Yolen

F

Fall: An Alphabet Acrostic by Steven Schnur
The Farm Alphabet Book by Jane Miller
The Flower Alphabet Book by Jerry Pallotta
The Frog Alphabet Book by Jerry Pallotta
The Furry Alphabet Book by Jerry Pallotta

G

G is for Galaxy: An Out of This World Alphabet by Cathy Collison and Janis Campbell
A Gardener's Alphabet by Mary Azarian
A Gull's Story, A Tale of Learning about Life, the Shore, and the ABCs by Frank Finale

H

H Is for Hoosier: An Indiana Alphabet by
Cynthia Furlong Reynolds
The Handmade Alphabet by Laura Rankin
H is for Horse: An Equestrian Alphabet by
Mike Ulmer

I

I is for Idea: An Inventions Alphabet by Marcia
Schonberg
I Spy: An Alphabet in Art (I Spy Series) by
Lucy Micklethwait
The Icky Bug Alphabet Book by Jerry Pallotta
I is for Iowa by Mary Ann Gensicke

J

Jambo Means Hello, a Swahili Alphabet Book
by Muriel Feelings
Journey Around New York from A to Z
by Martha Zschock
The Jet Alphabet Book by Jerry Pallotta
J is for Jump Shot: A Basketball Alphabet
by Mike Ulmer

K

*Miss Bindergarten Gets Ready for Kinder-
garten* by Joseph Slate

L

L Is for Last Frontier: An Alaska Alphabet
by Carol Crane
L is for Lincoln: An Illinois Alphabet by
Kathy-Jo Wargin
L is for Lobster: A Maine Alphabet by Cynthia
Furlong Reynolds
L Is for Lone Star: A Texas Alphabet by
Carol Crane

M

*M is for Magnolia: A Mississippi Alphabet
Book Edition 1,* by Michael Shoulders
M is for Maple: A Canadian Alphabet by
Michael Ulmer
M is for Maple Syrup: A Vermont Alphabet by
Cynthia Furlong Reynolds
M is for Melody: A Music Alphabet by
Kathy-Jo Wargin
*M is for Mountain State: A West Virginia
Alphabet* by Maryann McCabe Riehle
A Mountain Alphabet by Margriet Ruurs

N

Many Nations-An Alphabet of Native America
by Joseph Bruchac
Navajo ABC by Luci Tapahanso and
Eleanor Schick

O

The Ocean Alphabet Book by Jerry Pallotta

P

P Is for Palmetto: A South Carolina Alphabet
by Carol Crane
P is for Passport: A World Alphabet by Devin
Scillian
P is for Pilgrim: A Thanksgiving Alphabet by
Carol Crane
P is for Peach: A Georgia Alphabet by Carol
Crane
Paddington's ABC by Michael Bond
Peter Rabbit's ABC by Beatrix Potter

Q

Eight Hands Round - A Patchwork Alphabet by
Ann Whitford Paul
Q is for Duck: An Alphabet Guessing Game by
Mary Elting

R

Rainy Day Alphabet Book by Jackie Posner
A Walk in the Rainforest by Kristin Joy Pratt

S

S Is for Show Me: A Missouri Alphabet by
Judy Young
S Is for South Carolina by E. J. Sullivan
S is for Sunshine: A Florida Alphabet by
Carol Crane
Sharkabet: A Sea of Sharks from A to Z
by Ray Troll
Spring: An Alphabet Acrostic by Steven
Schnur

T

T is for Texas by Cynthia Furlong Reynolds
Tomorrow's Alphabet by George Shannon

U

The Ultimate Alphabet by Mike Wilks
The Underwater Alphabet Book by
Jerry Pallotta

V

V Is for Volunteer: A Tennessee Alphabet by
Michael Shoulders

The Victory Garden Alphabet Book by
Jerry Pallotta

W

W Is for Wind: A Weather Alphabet by
Pat Michaels

W Is for Wisconsin by Dori Hillestad Butler

W Is for World: A Round-the-World ABC by
Kate Cave and Oxfam

X

The EXtinct Alphabet Book by Jerry Pallotta

Y

The Yucky Reptile Alphabet Book by
Jerry Pallotta

Z

The Z Was Zapped by Chris Van Allsberg

Z Is for Zamboni: A Hockey Alphabet by
Matt Napier

Z Is for Zookeeper: A Zoo Alphabet by
Marie and Roland Smith

Appendix A
Developmental Writing Scale
Beginning Writers

READ DESCRIPTORS FOR EACH LEVEL OF THE BEGINNING WRITER'S SCALE FROM BOTTOM TO TOP

Level 8:   ___Child writes the start of a story.
___Mistakes in grammar, mechanics, and usage may detract from clarity and meaning.
___Child begins to use more conventional spelling.
___At least two thoughts follow one another in logical sequence.

Level 7:   ___Child begins to use capitalization and simple punctuation (e.g. period) often in a random fashion.
___Child uses both phonics and sight strategies to spell words.
___Child writes some sentences related to topic and some not related to topic.
___Child writes short, simple sentences that are not in a pattern form.
___Child writes sentences of more than 4 words following a pattern.

Level 6:   ___Child begins to write 2 or 3 sentences using a simple pattern form of 3 or 4 words (e.g. I love…).
___Child uses invented spelling and some conventional spelling.
___Child writes a single, factual, understandable sentence independently.

Level 5:   ___Child begins to use spaces between words.
___Child uses familiar words and invented spelling words to convey short, simple message.
___Child uses initial consonants to represent words.
___Child uses labels for his pictures.
___Child writes familiar words.

Level 4:   ___Child writes letters in word grouping and can read it back.
___Child writes letters to convey a message and can read it back.
___Child dictates one or more sentences, copies it, reads it back, and can still remember it the next day.
___Child dictates one or more sentences, copies it, and can read it back.
___Child dictates one or more sentences and copies it.**

Level 3:   ___Letters don't match sounds.
___Child writes alphabet letter strings.
___Child copies words he/she sees around the room.
___Copies dictated words.**

Level 2:   ___Alphabet letters and mock letters are in a line across the page.
___Child writes alphabet and mock letters around the page.
___Child writes mock letters.
___Child pretends to write.

Level 1:   ___Child draws a picture in response to a prompt and can verbalize about it.
___Child draws a picture and can talk about his picture.
___Child draws a picture, but cannot verbalize about picture.
___Child attempts to write in scribbles or draws patterns.
___Uncontrolled scribbling.   **[start here and read up]**

Winsand, J. (1996). *Blackburn-Cramp developmental writing scale: Beginning writers.* Syllabus Material from I&L 2231, Elementary Language Arts Methods. 1996, University of Pittsburgh, PA. Reprinted by permission of Jean Winsand Estate.

Extending Writer's Scale (Continuation of Beginning Writer's Scale)
Descriptors for Conventions of Writing

Element	Level 9	Level 10	Level 11	Level 12	Level 13	Level 14
Organization	Piece has beginning and middle but weak ending	Piece has beginning, middle, but weak ending; paragraphs are organized around a topic sentence	Piece has beginning, middle, end; paragraphs organized around a topic sentence	Similar to previous level	———————→	Begins use of foreshadowing; builds suspense
Sentence structure	Run-on sentences, mostly short, simple sentences using "because" and noun-verb beginnings of sentences	Fewer run-on sentences; mostly short, simple sentences w/n-vb beginnings; 1 or a few complex sentences with dependent clauses	Short, simple sentences w/n-vb beginnings; some different sentence beginnings, Ex: Suddenly; some complex & compound sentences	Uses variety of sentences, statements, questions, and exclamations	Uses sentence structure to fit mood of piece	———————→
Mechanics; usage	Mistakes do not detract from meaning; uses some periods & capital letters	Consistent use of periods; sometimes use of quotation marks, exclamation pts; indents paragraphs	Consistent use of standard n-vb agreement; uses commas in a series	Consistent use of periods, question marks, capitals, including proper nouns	———————→	———————→
Logical sequence	Most or all thoughts follow logical sequence	Same as level 9	All thoughts follow a logical sequence	———————→	———————→	———————→
Focus	Piece is focused on one idea	———————→	———————→	———————→	———————→	———————→
Sense of time and place	Limited mostly to repeated use of 'then'	Uses other words to describe place & time, 'When we got to…' 'By the time we…'	———————→	———————→	Writer provides detailed, believable description of a given place and/or time	———————→
Details	Factual details using mostly noun phrases; sounds like a list	Some details are related to each other & seem to flow together	Begins to paint word pictures; details give story credibility, they support the time setting of story	———————→	———————→	———————→
Length	Essentially 1 paragraph	Usually more than one paragraph	———————→	———————→	Fully elaborated topic; longer & greater # of paragraphs, e.g. 5 or more	———————→
Narrator	Almost all in first person (I, me)	Some 3rd person narration (he/she)	———————→	———————→	———————→	———————→
Word choice	Very basic use of words, i.e. nouns, verbs	Beginning use of adjectives	Frequent use of adjectives	Effective word choice evokes creative use of lang; strengthens writer's message; use of a few advanced adj's and/or adverbs	Consistent use of advanced adjectives, adverbs, verbs, etc.	———————→
Use of dialogue	Not used	Begins to use dialogue but no use of quotation marks	Uses quotation marks correctly most of the time	———————→	———————→	Uses dialogue to advance plot & develop characters
Emotions/ Humor/ Imagery	None elicited	Some simple, original images used, i.e. "It looked like a castle"	Some sense of humor, sadness, or other emotions, i.e. "Her long lost buddy…"	Feeling tone maintained from beginning to end	———————→	———————→
Audience/ Engaging Reader	No sense of audience	Captures reader's interest at times but doesn't sustain it	Captures & sustains reader's interest	———————→	———————→	———————→

A Description of Levels 1–8 from the Blackburn-Cramp Developmental Writing Scale

Level 1

In **level 1** writing, at first the child may pick up a crayon in his/her fist and scribble on a sheet of paper. The child may show it to an adult and say, "Look at my picture, Mommy!" When Mommy asks, "Tell me about your picture," the child probably cannot produce a description that coordinates with the picture. Toward the latter part of level 1, the child is able to draw a picture in response to a suggestion and is able to talk about the picture. What are some of the characteristics of a level 1 writer that you see in **example 1?**

Level 2

As a child moves into **level 2** writing, he/she has watched parents write letters and make grocery lists. The child begins to write mock letters at this stage after observing parental modeling. Later in this stage, the child progresses by writing both recognizable letters and mock letters in a line as he/she continues to see parents writing for authentic purposes. The child may write from left to right or vice versa on a line. Which letters do you think are the first ones a child learns to write? Do you see a progression toward more recognizable letters in **example 2?**

Level 3

In **level 3** writing, the child is able to copy words that he/she dictates to the teacher who writes them down. In addition, the child is able to copy words from environmental print. Parents often think their children have become amazingly literate at this stage. However, it is a type of mimicry that is typical at this level. At this stage, the letters typically do not match their sounds. What aspects of level 3 writing are conveyed in **example 3**?

Level 4

Level 4 represents a huge conceptual leap for the child. At this stage, the child understands that writing represents spoken language which can be written to convey a message. Early in this stage, the child can dictate a sentence or two, copy it, and read it. Later in this stage, the child can read the sentence(s) back at that time and on the next day. At the end of this stage, the child progresses to independent writing as he/she understands the concept of word boundaries. The child writes groups of words to convey a message and is able to read it back. Given what you see in **example 4,** how would you characterize this child's progression in level 4? What specific characteristics do you note in relation to this child's progression through this level?

Level 5

At the beginning of **level 5,** the child writes words that are familiar to him/her and often labels pictures. When writing sentences, the child often writes the initial consonant of each word, unless the word is one he/she knows. Toward the end of this stage, the child uses a combination of familiar words and invented (temporary) spelling to convey short, simple messages. Often, one will see the child writing words as a list to convey what he/she has drawn. What characteristics of level 5 are prevalent in **example 5?**

Level 6

During **level 6,** the child continues to progress as he/she writes independently, producing factual and understandable sentences using a combination of invented (temporary) and conventional spelling. At the end of this stage, the child can produce two or three sentences, following a pattern which may be designated by the teacher or created by the child. In **example 6,** what evidence do you see to classify it as level 6 writing?

Level 7

At the beginning of **level 7,** the child continues to refine his/her knowledge of letters and sounds and writes sentences of more than four words following a pattern. Soon the child is able to write sentences without using a pattern as a springboard for ideas and expression. The child writes brief stories that sometimes may or may not stay on topic. Later in this level, the child continues to refine his/her use of both phonics and sight strategies as he/she spells words. Finally, the child begins to make use of early knowledge of capitalization and punctuation, although often in a random fashion. What progression do you see in **example 7,** and what does this tell you about the child's development? How does this compare with example 6? Do you think the child generated the spelling(s) of these words? Explain your perspective.

Level 8

Level 8 writers move from writing isolated sentences that may relate to a topic to sentences that are connected in a more smooth progression of ideas. During this stage, the child uses more conventional spelling; however, mistakes in grammar and usage may distract from the meaning of the piece. At the end of this stage, the child is able to write the beginning of a story. What characteristics of level 8 writing are evident in **example 8?** Based on this child's writing sample, what are your conclusions about what this child knows and understands about writing conventions? If you were to conference with this child, what would you consider about what this child knows and understands about language and writing? What areas of writing would you focus on to help this child advance to the next level?

Please keep in mind that both the Beginning Writer's Scale and the Extending Writers' Scale are developmental, and the child's writing may not demonstrate all the characteristics listed in a given level. For example, *most, but not all* descriptors of Level 7 need apply to a piece for that piece to be considered a Level 7. Teacher judgment is essential in deciding the level that best describes a certain piece. We have found that use of the descriptors in conjunction with use of the exemplars results in highly reliable scoring.

**Dictate: The child tells someone else what he wants to write. That person writes it for the child. The child then copies on his/her paper. Even though dictation does not take place during an independent writing sample collection, dictation is an important stage of development which occurs frequently during ongoing writing workshops.

Level 1

Level 2

red broWngreenbl
rellowblue
orange
purple broWn

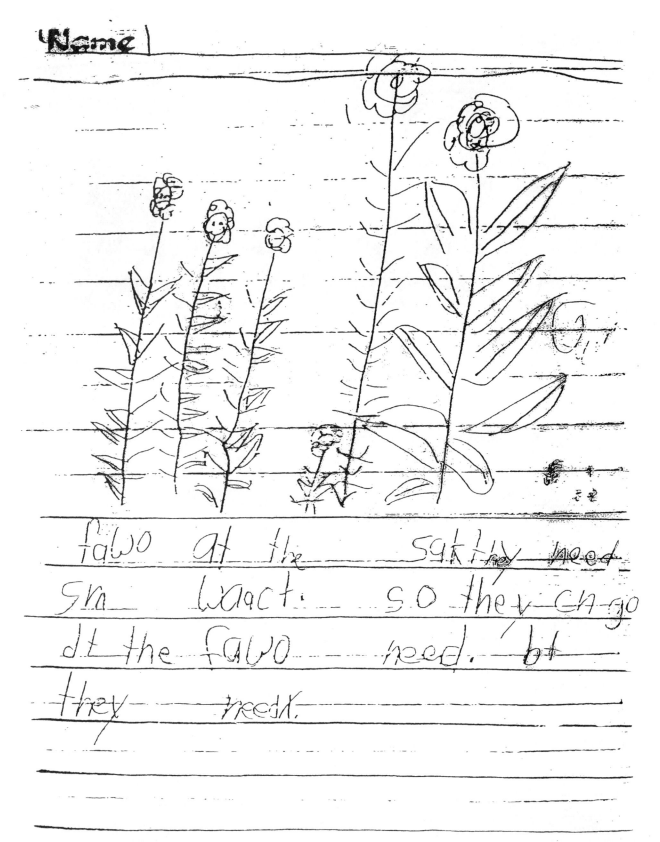

fawo at the sqktly need
sm waact. so they ch go
dt the fawo need. bt
they reedx.

Level 4

Name

mom
sister
brother
dad
cat
i dog

name

I Love you dog
I Love you MoM
I Love you Cat
I Love you Michelle
I Love you

Level 6

112

I am special because I love School
I am special because I love writer
I am special because I learn.
I am special because I help.
I am Special because I have a twin sister
I am Special because I have family.
I am Special because I can read.
I am Special because I had a baby broth

The most fun I ever had was when I wa

Suming wif My mom and my dad.

My mom nos hal to sum.

I nos i hal to sum to.

I had a lot of fun.

Level 8

The Impact of Writing on a Child's Future

It is important for teachers to convey the value of emergent writers' interests and imaginary explorations as they provide writing opportunities in the classroom. These early reading and writing experiences may have a significant impact on a child's future decisions. For instance, it is evident from the writing examples on the following pages that Noelle was always intrigued by horses. As a two-year-old, she experienced her first horseback ride which set the stage for her life-long interest, both personally and professionally.

Noelle's teachers nurtured her enthusiasm for horses which manifested in her writing and reading. Through writer's workshop, teachers promoted Noelle's enjoyment of writing by giving her opportunities to express her love of horses. During writing workshop, Noelle's experiences in writing reflected her experiences in play. For example, when Noelle was four and five years old, she often spent weekends with a close friend. Both children stayed in character "as horses" during the entire weekend, eating, whinnying, and galloping on all fours! In kindergarten, Noelle's writing actually became an extension of these experiences and every opportunity she had to be with horses.

Writing was not just a part of writing workshop in Noelle's early elementary grade experiences. Her teachers started each day with free writing in journals. As soon as students arrived, they had an opportunity to express their thoughts. When you look at the examples on the following pages, note the characteristics from her journal entries that align with the Blackburn-Cramp Developmental Writing Scale. What did Noelle understand about language in each example taken from her first grade year in school? What stage of writing development would you designate for each of these examples? How did her writing develop over time from September 9th to February 21st? Based on what you know about first graders' writing development, what do you consider the strengths of Noelle's writing, and what areas would you focus on to enhance her writing development?

Example 1: Journal sample from week two of the school year

Example 2: Journal sample from week six of the school year

Example 3: Journal sample from the sixth month of the school year

As Noelle grew and continued her development as a writer, she began to explore different genres of writing, but her topics usually remained the same. However, in fourth grade, as Noelle continued to write stories about horses, she began to use writing as a means to understand math, a subject that often presented challenges. On her own volition, Noelle began to convert her math problems into story problems as a means to make them more understandable. By doing so, she was able to solve the problems. Her fourth grade teacher was so amazed by this innovation that she copied Noelle's story problems and gave them to all the students to solve. Her fourth grade teacher said that she expected to see Noelle's name on the covers of children's books in the future.

In middle school, she began to write poetry, delving into more thought-provoking issues associated with horses and horse ownership. She even wrote a profound poem in which she entered the minds of various horses as they were being transported to a slaughter house. Noelle actually majored in Equine Science in college, with a minor in creative writing. Now she enjoys working with her own horse and training other young horse enthusiasts to ride as well! Writing remains an important part of her life. In fact, she is currently writing her memoirs!

9-9-88

IISRDYARNAHO

I'm riding on a horse.

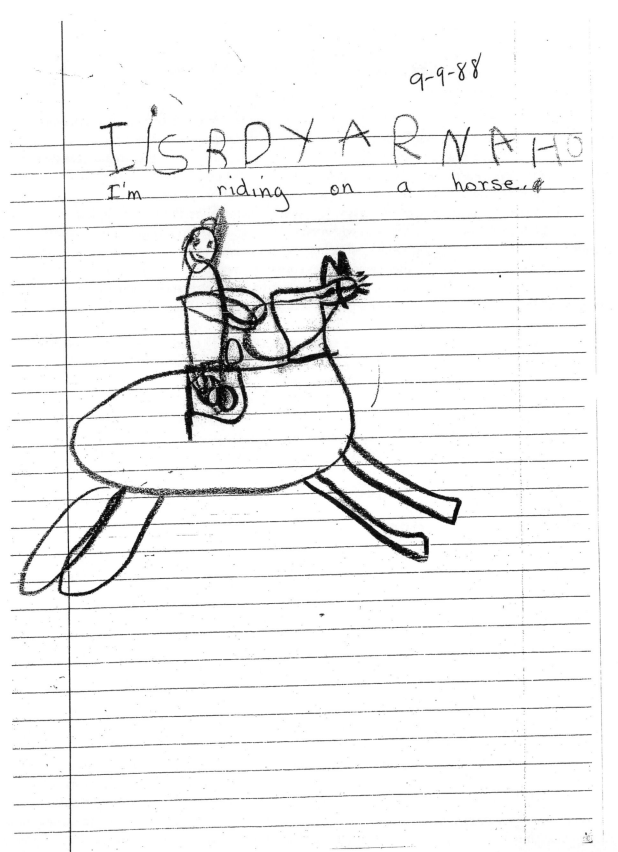

Example 1

116

10-6-88

I IM r IDYN
I am riding

ON
on

A
UNICONr
unicorn

Example 2

117

2-21-89

casey is coming
to Watch as atare
our
house at 6oc.
beasse mos at
because Mom's
Playcract.
practice

Example 3

Appendix B
Measuring Attitude Toward Reading: A New Tool for Teachers

In 1762, the philosopher Rousseau speculated that any method of teaching reading would suffice given adequate motivation on the part of the learner. While present-day educators might resist such a sweeping pronouncement, the importance of attitude is nevertheless widely recognized. The Commission on Reading in its summary of research (Anderson, Hiebert, Scott, & Wilkinson, 1985) concluded that "becoming a skilled reader requires...learning that written material can be interesting" (p. 18). Smith (1988) observed that "the emotional response to reading...is the primary reason most readers read, and probably the primary reason most nonreaders do not read" (p. 177). Wixson and Lipson (in press) acknowledge that "the student's attitude toward reading is a central factor affecting reading performance." These conclusions are based on a long history of research in which attitude and achievement have been consistently linked (e.g., Purves & Beach, 1972; Walberg & Tsai, 1985).

The recent emphasis on enhanced reading proficiency has often ignored the important role played by children's attitudes in the process of becoming literate. Athey (1985) suggested that one reason for this tendency is that the affective aspects of reading tend to be ill-defined and to involve "shadowy variables" (p. 527) difficult to conceptualize, measure, and address instructionally.

The focus of recent research and development in assessment has been comprehension rather than attitude. Some progress has been made in the development of individually administered, qualitative instruments, but quantitative group surveys, which form a natural complement to qualitative approaches, are often poorly documented in terms of desirable psychometric attributes, such as normative frames of reference and evidence of reliability and validity. Our purpose was to produce a public-domain instrument that would remedy these shortcomings and enable teachers to estimate attitude levels efficiently and reliably. This article presents that instrument along with a discussion of its development and suggestions for its use.

Development of the Scale

Several important criteria were established to guide the development of the instrument. The

Appendix from McKenna, M. C. & Kearn, D. J. (1990, May). Measuring attitude toward reading: A new tool for teachers. *The Reading Teacher, 43*(9) 626–639. Reprinted with permission of the International Reading Association. The GARFIELD character is incorporated in this test with the permission of UNIVERSAL PRESS SYNDICATE. All rights reserved.

authors agreed that the survey must (a) have a large-scale normative frame of reference; (b) comprise a set of items selected on the basis of desirable psychometric properties; (c) have empirically documented reliability and validity; (d) be applicable to all elementary students, Grades 1 through 6; (e) possess a meaningful, attention-getting, student-friendly response format; (f) be suitable for brief group administration; and (g) comprise separate subscales for recreational and academic reading. We knew of no instrument that possessed all of these characteristics.

A pictorial format was elected because of its natural appeal for children and because of its comprehensibility by the very young. An informal survey of more than 30 elementary teachers indicated that the comic strip character Garfield was more apt to be recognized by children in Grades 1 through 6 than any other. Jim Davis, who is the creator of Garfield, and United Features, his publisher, agreed to supply four black-line, camera-ready poses of Garfield, ranging from very happy to very upset, and to permit the resulting instrument to be copied and used by educators. (See the Elementary Reading Attitude Survey and scoring sheet prior to the Appendix at the end of this article.)

An even number of scale points avoids a neutral, central category which respondents often select in order to avoid committing themselves even when clear opinions exist (Nunnally, 1967). The use of four points was based on a substantial body of research suggesting that young children typically can discriminate among no more than five discrete bits of information simultaneously (e.g., Case & Khanna, 1981; Chi, 1978; Chi & Klahr, 1975; Nitko, 1983).

Several earlier surveys were used as models in the creation of an item pool from which the final set of items would be constructed (e.g., Estes, 1971; Heathington, 1979; Right to Read, 1976; Robinson & Good, 1987). A total of 39 items were developed, each related to one of two aspects of attitude: (a) attitude toward recre-ational reading (24 items) or (b) attitude toward academic reading (15 items). To establish a consistent, appropriate expectation on the part of the students, each item was worded with a uniform beginning: "How do you feel…."

This prototype instrument was then administered to 499 elementary students in a middle-sized midwestern U.S. school district. For each of the two item sets (recreational and academic), final sets of 10 items each were selected on the basis of inter-item correlation coefficients. The revised instrument was then administered at midyear to a national sample of over 18,000 children in Grades 1–6. Estimates of reliability, as well as evidence of validity, were based on this national sample. A complete description of the technical aspects of the survey appears in the Appendix.

Administering and Scoring the Survey

The Elementary Reading Attitude Survey (ERAS) can be given to an entire class in a matter of minutes, but, as with any normed instrument, it is important that the administration reflect as closely as possible the procedure used with the norming group. The administration procedures are presented in the "Directions for Use" information that accompanies the instrument itself. This process involves first familiarizing students with the instrument and with the purposes for giving it. The teacher next reads the items aloud twice as the students mark their responses.

Each item is then assigned 1, 2, 3, or 4 points, a "4" indicating the happiest (leftmost) Garfield. The scoring sheet that follows the instrument can be used to organize this process and record recreational, academic, and total scores, along with the percentile rank of each. The results are then ready for use.

Using the Survey

Collecting data about students is an empty exercise unless the information is used to plan instruction. Scores on the ERAS can be helpful in this process, but it is important to understand what they can and cannot do as well as how they relate to other sources of information.

Strengths and limitations. This survey provides quantitative estimates of two important aspects of children's attitudes toward reading. Like global measures of achievement, however, they can do little in themselves to identify the causes of poor attitude or to suggest instructional techniques likely to improve it. On the other hand, the instrument can be used to (a) make possible initial conjecture about the attitudes of specific students, (b) provide a convenient group profile of a class (or a larger unit), or (c) serve as a means of monitoring the attitudinal impact of instructional programs.

A classroom plan. A teacher might begin by administering the ERAS during the first few weeks of the school year. Class averages for recreational and academic reading attitude will enable the teacher to characterize the class generally on these two dimensions. Scores for individual students may suggest the need to further explore the nature, strength, and origins of their values and beliefs. This goal could be pursued through the use of individually conducted strategies such as structured interviews, open-ended sentence instruments, or interest inventories. Reed (1979) suggested using nonreactive measures as well, such as recorded teacher observations following reading instruction and reading-related activities. The combination of these techniques provides a variety of useful information that can be collected in portfolio fashion for individual students.

Survey results can be very useful in deciding what sorts of additional information to pursue. Four general response patterns are especially notable, and we will depict each of them with hypothetical students who are, in fact,

composites of many with whom we have worked.

Two profiles involve sizable differences (5 points or more) between recreational and academic scores. Jimmy, a third grader, has a recreational score of 29 and an academic score of 21. The difference suggests a stronger attitude toward reading for fun than for academic purposes. To an extent, this pattern is typical of third graders (compare the means in Table 2 in the Appendix), but not to the degree exhibited in Jimmy's case. Had both scores been higher, Jimmy's teacher might have been justified in disregarding the difference, but a score of 21 is low both in the criterial sense (it is close to the slightly frowning Garfield) and in a normative one (18th percentile rank). Examining the last 10 items of the survey one-by-one might prove helpful in forming hypotheses about which aspects are troublesome. These can then be tested by carefully observing Jimmy during reading instruction.

For Katy, a fifth grader, assume that the two scores are reversed. By virtue of her stronger attitude toward academic reading, Katy is somewhat atypical. Her academic score of 29 is quite strong in both a criterial sense (it is near the slightly smiling Garfield) and a normative sense (71st percentile rank). Her score of 21 in recreational reading attitude is cause for concern (13th percentile rank), but the strong academic score suggests that her disdain is not total and may be traceable to causes subject to intervention. Because items 1–10 are somewhat global in nature, it is unlikely that scrutinizing her responses will be very helpful. A nonthreatening chat about reading habits may be much more productive in helping her teacher identify Katy's areas of interest and even suggest a book or two. Katy may not have been exposed to a variety of interesting trade books.

Two other profiles involve differences between attitude and ability. These are very real possibilities that require careful attention

(Roettger, 1980). Consider Patrick, a second grader whose academic attitude score is 28 and who has been placed in a low-ability group by his teacher. Patrick's relatively positive score (near the smiling Garfield) may encourage his teacher, for it is apt to be higher than others in his reading group. However, more than half of his second-grade peers across the country have stronger attitudes toward reading in school. Data from this study document a widening attitudinal gap between low- and high-ability children as they move through school. Patrick's teacher should be concerned about the likely effects of another frustrating year on his attitude toward instruction. Teaching methods and instructional materials should be scrutinized.

Ironically, the same conclusion might be reached for Deborah, a sixth-grade student of extraordinary ability. Her academic attitude score, however, is only 17, which is quite negative, whether one looks to its position among the pictures or notes that it represents a percentile rank of 11. If Deborah's recreational score were substantially higher, her teacher would be correct in wondering whether the instruction she is receiving is adequately engaging. As with Jimmy, an inspection of her responses to items 11–20 could be helpful, followed by a nonintrusive reading interview and tactful observation. On the other hand, suppose that Deborah's recreational score were also 17. This would place her total score (34) at the 5th percentile rank and suggest a strong disinclination to read despite the ability to do so. This would warrant action on the part of an insightful teacher who is willing to make instructional and leisure reading attractive.

Examples of this nature illustrate how the Elementary Reading Attitude Survey can enter into the process of instructional planning, especially near the beginning of a school year. As the year draws to a close, the survey can again be given, this time to monitor any attitudinal changes of the class as a whole. By comparing class averages from the beginning and end of the year, a teacher can gauge the movement of a class relative both to its own earlier position and to a national midyear average. Estimating year-long changes for individual students is a less reliable process and should only be attempted with regard to the standard error of measurement for a given subscale and grade level (see Table 2 in the Appendix). We recommend using twice the standard error to construct an adequate confidence interval. In other words, the pre/post difference would, in general, need to be 5 points or more on either the academic or recreational subscale before *any* real change could be assumed. On the total score, the pre/post change would need to be 7 or 8 points.

Conclusion

The instrument presented here builds on the strengths of its predecessors and, it is hoped, remedies some of their psychometric shortcomings. Its placement into the public domain by means of this article provides teachers with a tool that can be used with relative confidence to estimate the attitude levels of their students and initiate informal assessment efforts into the role attitude plays in students' development as readers.

Authors' Note

The authors wish to express their sincere thanks to Jim Davis for his Garfield illustrations and for his concern for children's literacy abilities.

References

Anderson, R.C., Hiebert, E.H., Scott, J.A., & Wilkinson, I.A.G. (1985). *Becoming a nation of readers: The report of the Commission on Reading.* Washington, DC: National Institute of Education.

Athey, I.J. (1985). Reading research in the affective domain. In H. Singer & R.B. Ruddell (Eds.), *Theoretical models and processes of reading* (3rd ed., pp. 527–557). Newark, DE: International Reading Association.

Case, R., & Khanna, F. (1981). The missing links: Stages in children's progression from sensorimotor to logical thought. In K.W. Fischer (Ed.), *Cognitive development (New directions for child development, No. 12)*. San Francisco: Jossey-Bass.

Chi, M.T. (1978). Knowledge structures and memory development. In R.S. Siegler (Ed.), *Children's thinking: What develops?* Hillsdale, NJ: Erlbaum.

Chi, M.T., & Klahr, D. (1975). Span and rate of apprehension in children and adults. *Journal of Experimental Psychology, 19*, 434–439.

Cronbach, L.J. (1951). Coefficient alpha and the internal structure of tests. *Psychometrika, 16*, 297–334.

Estes, T.H. (1971). A scale to measure attitudes toward reading. *Journal of Reading, 15*, 135–138.

Heathington, B.S. (1979). What to do about reading motivation in the middle school. *Journal of Reading, 22*, 709–713.

Nitko, A.J. (1983). *Educational tests and measurement: An introduction*. New York: Harcourt Brace Jovanovich.

Nunnally, J.C. (1967). *Psychometric theory*. New York: McGraw-Hill.

Purves, A.C., & Beach, R. (1972). *Literature and the reader: Research in response to literature, reading interests, and the teaching of literature*. Urbana, IL: National Council of Teachers of English.

Reed, K. (1979). Assessing affective responses to reading: A multi-measurement model. *Reading World, 19*, 149–156.

Right to Read Office. (1976). *Reading interest/attitude scale*. Washington, DC: United States Office of Education.

Robinson, R., & Good, T.L. (1987). *Becoming an effective reading teacher*. New York: Harper & Row.

Roettger, D. (1980). Elementary students' attitudes toward reading. *The Reading Teacher, 33*, 451–453.

Rousseau, J-J. (1762/1979). *Emile, or on education* (trans. A. Bloom). New York: Basic Books.

Smith, F. (1988). *Understanding reading: A psycholinguistic analysis of reading and learning to read* (4th ed.). Hillsdale, NJ: Erlbaum.

Statistical abstract of the United States. (1989). Washington, DC: Bureau of Census, Department of Commerce.

Walberg, H.J., & Tsai, S. (1985). Correlates of reading achievement and attitude: A national assessment study. *Journal of Educational Research, 78*, 159–167.

Wixson, K.K., & Lipson, M.Y. (in press). *Reading diagnosis and remediation*. Glenview, IL: Scott, Foresman.

Appendix
Technical Aspects of the Elementary Reading Attitude Survey

The norming project

    To create norms for the interpretation of scores, a large-scale study was conducted in late January 1989, at which time the survey was administered to 18,138 students in Grades 1–6. A number of steps were taken to achieve a sample that was sufficiently stratified (i.e., reflective of the American population) to allow confident generalizations. Children were drawn from 95 school districts in 38 U.S. states. The number of girls exceeded by only 5 the number of boys. Ethnic distribution of the sample was also close to that of the U.S. population (*Statistical abstract of the United States*, 1989). The proportion of blacks (9.5%) was within 3% of the national proportion, while the proportion of Hispanics (6.2%) was within 2%.

    Percentile ranks at each grade for both subscales and the full scale are presented in Table 1. These data can be used to compare individual students' scores with the national sample and they can be interpreted like achievement-test percentile ranks.

Table 1
Mid-year percentile ranks by grade and scale

Raw Scr	Grade 1 Rec Aca Tot	Grade 2 Rec Aca Tot	Grade 3 Rec Aca Tot	Grade 4 Rec Aca Tot	Grade 5 Rec Aca Tot	Grade 6 Rec Aca Tot
80	99	99	99	99	99	99
79	95	96	98	99	99	99
78	93	95	97	98	99	99
77	92	94	97	98	99	99
76	90	93	96	97	98	99
75	88	92	95	96	98	99
74	86	90	94	95	97	99
73	84	88	92	94	97	98
72	82	86	91	93	96	98
71	80	84	89	91	95	97
70	78	82	86	89	94	96
69	75	79	84	88	92	95
68	72	77	81	86	91	93
67	69	74	79	83	89	92
66	66	71	76	80	87	90
65	62	69	73	78	84	88
64	59	66	70	75	82	86
63	55	63	67	72	79	84
62	52	60	64	69	76	82
61	49	57	61	66	73	79
60	46	54	58	62	70	76
59	43	51	55	59	67	73
58	40	47	51	56	64	69
57	37	45	48	53	61	66
56	34	41	44	48	57	62
55	31	38	41	45	53	58
54	28	35	38	41	50	55

Table 1
Mid-year percentile ranks by grade and scale (continued)

Raw Scr	Grade 1			Grade 2			Grade 3			Grade 4			Grade 5			Grade 6		
	Rec	Aca	Tot	Rec	Aca	Tot	Rec	Aca	Tot	Rec	Aca	Tot	Rec	Aca	Tot	Rec	Aca	Tot
53			25			32			34			38			46			52
52			22			29			31			35			42			48
51			20			26			28			32			39			44
50			18			23			25			28			36			40
49			15			20			23			26			33			37
48			13			18			20			23			29			33
47			12			15			17			20			26			30
46			10			13			15			18			23			27
45			8			11			13			16			20			25
44			7			9			11			13			17			22
43			6			8			9			12			15			20
42			5			7			8			10			13			17
41			5			6			7			9			12			15
40	99	99	4	99	99	5	99	99	6	99	99	7	99	99	10	99	99	13
39	92	91	3	94	94	4	96	97	6	97	98	6	98	99	9	99	99	12
38	89	88	3	92	92	3	94	95	4	95	97	5	96	98	8	97	99	10
37	86	85	2	88	89	2	90	93	3	92	95	4	94	98	7	95	99	8
36	81	79	2	84	85	2	87	91	2	88	93	3	91	96	6	92	98	7
35	77	75	1	79	81	1	81	88	2	84	90	3	87	95	4	88	97	6
34	72	69	1	74	78	1	75	83	2	78	87	2	82	93	4	83	95	5
33	65	63	1	68	73	1	69	79	1	72	83	2	77	90	3	79	93	4
32	58	58	1	62	67	1	63	74	1	66	79	1	71	86	3	74	91	3
31	52	53	1	56	62	1	57	69	0	60	75	1	65	82	2	69	87	2
30	44	49	1	50	57	0	51	63	0	54	70	1	59	77	1	63	82	2
29	38	44	0	44	51	0	45	58	0	47	64	1	53	71	1	58	78	1
28	32	39	0	37	46	0	38	52	0	41	58	1	48	66	1	51	73	1
27	26	34	0	31	41	0	33	47	0	35	52	1	42	60	1	46	67	1
26	21	30	0	25	37	0	26	41	0	29	46	0	36	54	0	39	60	1
25	17	25	0	20	32	0	21	36	0	23	40	0	30	49	0	34	54	0
24	12	21	0	15	27	0	17	31	0	19	35	0	25	42	0	29	49	0
23	9	18	0	11	23	0	13	26	0	14	29	0	20	37	0	24	42	0
22	7	14	0	8	18	0	9	22	0	11	25	0	16	31	0	19	36	0
21	5	11	0	6	15	0	6	18	0	9	20	0	13	26	0	15	30	0
20	4	9	0	4	11	0	5	14	0	6	16	0	10	21	0	12	24	0
19	2	7		2	8		3	11		5	13		7	17		10	20	
18	2	5		2	6		2	8		3	9		6	13		5	18	
17	1	4		1	5		1	5		2	7		4	9		6	11	
16	1	3		1	3		1	4		2	5		3	6		4	8	
15	0	2		0	2		0	3		1	3		2	4		3	6	
14	0	2		0	1		0	1		1	2		1	2		1	3	
13	0	1		0	1		0	1		0	1		1	2		1	2	
12	0	1		0	0		0	0		0	1		0	1		0	1	
11	0	0		0	0		0	0		0	0		0	0		0	0	
10	0	0		0	0		0	0		0	0		0	0		0	0	

Appendix
Technical Aspects of the Elementary Reading Attitude Survey (continued)

Reliability

Cronbach's alpha, a statistic developed primarily to measure the internal consistency of attitude scales (Cronbach, 1951), was calculated at each grade level for both subscales and for the composite score. These coefficients ranged from .74 to .89 and are presented in Table 2.

It is interesting that with only two exceptions, coefficients were .80 or higher. These were for the recreational subscale at Grades 1 and 2. It is possible that the stability of young children's attitudes toward leisure reading grows with their decoding ability and familiarity with reading as a pastime.

Table 2
Descriptive statistics and internal consistency measures

Grade	N	Recreational Subscale				Academic Subscale				Full Scale (Total)			
		M	SD	S_eM	Alpha[a]	M	SD	S_eM	Alpha	M	SD	S_eM	Alpha
1	2,518	31.0	5.7	2.9	.74	30.1	6.8	3.0	.81	61.0	11.4	4.1	.87
2	2,974	30.3	5.7	2.7	.78	28.8	6.7	2.9	.81	59.1	11.4	3.9	.88
3	3,151	30.0	5.6	2.5	.80	27.8	6.4	2.8	.81	57.8	10.9	3.8	.88
4	3,679	29.5	5.8	2.4	.83	26.9	6.3	2.6	.83	56.5	11.0	3.6	.89
5	3,374	28.5	6.1	2.3	.86	25.6	6.0	2.5	.82	54.1	10.8	3.6	.89
6	2,442	27.9	6.2	2.2	.87	24.7	5.8	2.5	.81	52.5	10.6	3.5	.89
All	18,138	29.5	5.9	2.5	.82	27.3	6.6	2.7	.83	56.8	11.3	3.7	.89

[a] Cronbach's alpha (Cronbach, 1951).

Validity

Evidence of construct validity was gathered by several means. For the recreational subscale, students in the national norming group were asked (a) whether a public library was available to them and (b) whether they currently had a library card. Those to whom libraries were available were separated into two groups (those with and without cards) and their recreational scores were compared. Cardholders had significantly higher ($p < .001$) recreational scores ($M = 30.0$) than noncardholders ($M = 28.9$), evidence of the subscale's validity in that scores varied predictably with an outside criterion.

A second test compared students who presently had books checked out from their school library versus students who did not. The comparison was limited to children whose teachers reported not requiring them to check out books. The means of the two groups varied significantly ($p < .001$), and children with books checked out scored higher ($M = 29.2$) than those who had no books checked out ($M = 27.3$).

A further test of the recreational subscale compared students who reported watching an average of less than 1 hour of television per night with students who reported watching more than 2 hours per night. The recreational mean for the low televiewing group (31.5) significantly exceeded ($p < .001$) the mean of the heavy televiewing group (28.6). Thus, the amount of television watched varied inversely with children's attitudes toward recreational reading.

The validity of the academic subscale was tested by examining the relationship of scores to reading ability. Teachers categorized norm-group children as having low, average, or high overall reading ability. Mean subscale scores of the high-ability readers ($M = 27.7$) significantly exceeded the mean of

Appendix
Technical Aspects of the Elementary Reading Attitude Survey (continued)

low-ability readers ($M = 27.0$, $p < .001$), evidence that scores were reflective of how the students truly felt about reading for academic purposes.

The relationship between the subscales was also investigated. It was hypothesized that children's attitudes toward recreational and academic reading would be moderately but not highly correlated. Facility with reading is likely to affect these two areas similarly, resulting in similar attitude scores. Nevertheless, it is easy to imagine children prone to read for pleasure but disenchanted with assigned reading and children academically engaged but without interest in reading outside of school. The inter-subscale correlation coefficient was .64, which meant that just 41% of the variance in one set of scores could be accounted for by the other. It is reasonable to suggest that the two subscales, while related, also reflect dissimilar factors—a desired outcome.

To tell more precisely whether the traits measured by the survey corresponded to the two sub-scales, factor analyses were conducted. Both used the unweighted least squares method of extraction and a varimax rotation. The first analysis permitted factors to be identified liberally (using a limit equal to the smallest eigenvalue greater than 1). Three factors were identified. Of the 10 items comprising the academic subscale, 9 loaded predominantly on a single factor while the 10th (item 13) loaded nearly equally on all three factors. A second factor was dominated by 7 items of the recreational subscale, while 3 of the recreational items (6, 9, and 10) loaded principally on a third factor. These items did, however, load more heavily on the second (recreational) factor than on the first (academic). A second analysis constrained the identification of factors to two. This time, with one exception, all items loaded cleanly on factors associated with the two subscales. The exception was item 13, which could have been interpreted as a recreational item and thus apparently involved a slight ambiguity. Taken together, the factor analyses produced evidence extremely supportive of the claim that the survey's two subscales reflect discrete aspects of reading attitude.

Elementary Reading Attitude Survey
Directions for use

The Elementary Reading Attitude Survey provides a quick indication of student attitudes toward reading. It consists of 20 items and can be administered to an entire classroom in about 10 minutes. Each item presents a brief, simply worded statement about reading, followed by four pictures of Garfield. Each pose is designed to depict a different emotional state, ranging from very positive to very negative.

Administration

Begin by telling students that you wish to find out how they feel about reading. Emphasize that this is *not* a test and that there are no "right" answers. Encourage sincerity.

Distribute the survey forms and, if you wish to monitor the attitudes of specific students, ask them to write their names in the space at the top. Hold up a copy of the survey so that the students can see the first page. Point to the picture of Garfield at the far left of the first item. Ask the students to look at this same picture on their own survey form. Discuss with them the mood Garfield seems to be in (very happy). Then move to the next picture and again discuss Garfield's mood (this time, a *little* happy). In the same way, move to the third and fourth pictures and talk about Garfield's moods—a little upset and very upset. It is helpful to point out the position of Garfield's *mouth*, especially in the middle two figures.

Explain that together you will read some statements about reading and that the students should think about how they feel about each statement. They should then circle the picture of Garfield that is closest to their own feelings. (Emphasize that the students should respond according to their own feelings, not as Garfield might respond!) Read each item aloud slowly and distinctly; then read it a second time while students are thinking. Be sure to read the item *number* and to remind students of page numbers when new pages are reached.

Scoring

To score the survey, count four points for each leftmost (happiest) Garfield circled, three for each slightly smiling Garfield, two for each mildly upset Garfield, and one point for each very upset (rightmost) Garfield. Three scores for each student can be obtained: the total for the first 10 items, the total for the second 10, and a composite total. The first half of the survey relates to attitude toward recreational reading; the second half relates to attitude toward academic aspects of reading.

Interpretation

You can interpret scores in two ways. One is to note informally where the score falls in regard to the four nodes of the scale. A total score of 50, for example, would fall about mid-way on the scale, between the slightly happy and slightly upset figures, therefore indicating a relatively indifferent overall attitude toward reading. The other approach is more formal. It involves converting the raw scores into percentile ranks by means of Table 1. Be sure to use the norms for the right grade level and to note the column headings (Rec = recreational reading, Aca = academic reading, Tot = total score). If you wish to determine the average percentile rank for your class, average the raw scores first; then use the table to locate the percentile rank corresponding to the raw score mean. Percentile ranks cannot be averaged directly.

Elementary Reading Attitude Survey Scoring Sheet

Student Name_____

Teacher_____

Grade_____ Administration Date_____

```
                      Scoring Guide
      4 points      Happiest Garfield
      3 points      Slightly smiling Garfield
      2 points      Mildly upset Garfield
      1 point       Very upset Garfield
```

Recreational reading   Academic reading

1. _____   1. _____

2. _____   2. _____

3. _____   3. _____

4. _____   4. _____

5. _____   5. _____

6. _____   6. _____

7. _____   7. _____

8. _____   8. _____

9. _____   9. _____

10. _____   10. _____

Raw Score: _____   Raw Score: _____

Full scale raw score (Recreational + Academic) . . . . _____

Percentile ranks . . . . Recreational [   ]

. . . . Academic [   ]

. . . . Full scale [   ]

Elementary Reading Attitude Survey

School_____ Grade_____ Name_____

Please circle the picture that describes how you feel when you read a book.

1. How do you feel when you read a book on a rainy Saturday?

2. How do you feel when you read a book in school during free time?

3. How do you feel about reading for fun at home?

4. How do you feel about getting a book for a present?

Please circle the picture that describes how you feel when you read a book.

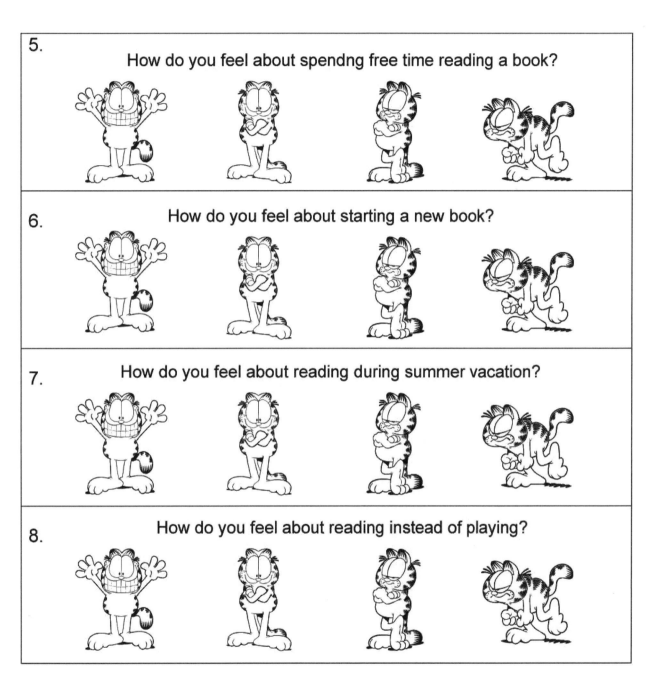

5. How do you feel about spendng free time reading a book?

6. How do you feel about starting a new book?

7. How do you feel about reading during summer vacation?

8. How do you feel about reading instead of playing?

Page 2

Please circle the picture that describes how you feel when you read a book.

9. How do you feel about going to a bookstore?

10. How do you feel about reading different kinds of books?

11. How do you feel when a teacher asks you questions about what you read?

12. How do you feel about reading workbook pages and worksheets?

Page 3

Please circle the picture that describes how you feel when you read a book.

13. How do you feel about reading in school?

14. How do you feel about reading your school books?

15. How do you feel about learning from a book?

16. How do you feel when it's time for reading in class?

Page 4

Please circle the picture that describes how you feel when you read a book.

17. How do you feel about stories you read in reading class?

18. How do you feel when you read out loud in class?

19. How do you feel about using a dictionary?

20. How do you feel about taking a reading test?

Page 5

134